SMAS

DISMAS

First published in 2020 by
Amerigo, s.r.o. – edition Citadelle, Poděbradská 56/186, 180 66 Prague 9, Czech Republic
www.citadelle.cz
Printed and bound in the Czech Republic

British Library Cataloguing in Publication Data
A catalogue record for this book is available from the British Library

All Scripture quotations are from the *Revised Standard Version of the Holy Bible*,
Published in New York, Glasgow, & Toronto by William Collins Sons & Co. Ltd.

Front jacket: *Crucifixion fresco* (1442) – Fra Angelico, Convent of San Marco,
Florence, Italy, © Photograph by Daniel Res

ISBN 978-80-907311-3-4

CONTENTS

LIST OF ILLUSTRATIONS

1) Sculptured head of the Emperor Tiberius – 1St Century AD – Archaeological Museum of Istanbul, Turkey,©Wikimedia Commons, https://commons.wikimedia.org/wiki/File:Tiberius_portrait_Istanbul_Archaeological_Museum_-_inv._5555_T_01.jpg

2) Christ Carrying the Cross (1500–1535) – Follower of Hieronymous Bosch, Museum of Fine Arts, Ghent, Belgium, ©Wikimedia Commons, https://commons.wikimedia.org/wiki/File:Hieronymus_Bosch_055.jpg

3) Via Dolorosa sign, Jersusalem, Israel ©Wikimedia Commons, https://commons.wikimedia.org/wiki/File:Via_Dolorosa_street_sign_(Jerusalem_2013)_(8682155535).jpg

4) The Raising of the Cross (1524) – Jorg Breu the Elder, Museum of Fine Arts, Budapest, Hungary, ©Wikimedia Commons, https://commons.wikimedia.org/wiki/File:J%C3%B6rg_Breu_d._%C3%84._-_Crucifixion_-_WGA03180.jpg

5) Crucifixion of Christ/Wilten Crucifixion (1435) – Unknown Tyrolean Painter, Kunsthistoriche Museum, Vienna, Austria, ©Wikimedia Commons, https://commons.wikimedia.org/wiki/File:Tiroler_Maler_-_Kreuzigung_Christi_(%22Wiltener_Kreuzigung%22)_-_4915_-_Belvedere.jpg

6) Crucifixion (1946) – George Russell Drysdale, © Art Gallery of New South Wales/Gift in memory of Hugh Alexander McClure Smith C.V.O. by his wife/ Bridgeman Images

7) Landscape with snow and the Crucifixion (1599) – Karel van Mander, Private Collection, ©Wikimedia Commons, https://commons.wikimedia.org/wiki/File:Karel_van_Mander_(I)_-_Landscape_with_snow_and_the_Crucifixion.jpg

8) Crucifixion (1880) – Thomas Eakins, Philadelphia Museum of Art, Philadelphia, USA, ©Wikimedia Commons, https://commons.wikimedia.org/wiki/File:Thomas_Eakins_-_The_Crucifixion_(1880).jpg

9) Crucifixion (1912) – Jindřich Průcha, National Gallery, Prague, Czech Republic, ©Wikimedia Commons, https://commons.wikimedia.org/wiki/File:Jind%C5%99ich_Prucha_-_Crucifixion.jpg

10) The Crucifixion, Les Très Riches Heures du duc de Berry, Folio 152v, The Condé Museum, Chantilly, France, ©Wikimedia Commons, https://commons.wikimedia.org/wiki/File:Folio_152v_-_The_Crucifixion.jpg

11) Crucifixion fresco (1513) – Gaudenzio Ferrari, The Church of Our Lady of the Graces, Varalla Sesia, Piedmont, Italy, ©Wikimedia Commons, https://commons.wikimedia.org/wiki/File:Gaudenzio_Ferrari,_Crucifixion,_1513,_fresco,_S._Maria_delle_Grazie,_Varallo_Sesia.jpg

12) The Crucifixion, Church of Debra Berhan Selassie, Gondar, Ethiopia © Wikimedia Commons, https://commons.wikimedia.org/wiki/File:The_Crucifiction_(2427079194).jpg

13) Christ and the Good Thief (circa 1561) – Titian, The National Art Gallery of Bologna, Italy, © Wikimedia Commons, https://commons.wikimedia.org/wiki/File:Titian_-_Christ_and_the_Good_Thief_-_WGA22832.jpg

14) Crucifixion (circa 1459) - Andrea Mantegna, The Louvre Museum, Paris, France, © Wikimedia Commons, https://commons.wikimedia.org/wiki/File:Mantegna,_Andrea_-_crucifixion_-_Louvre_from_Predella_San_Zeno_Altarpiece_Verona.jpg

15) Crucifixion (circa 1330) - Giotto di Bondone, The Louvre Museum, Paris, France, © Wikimedia Commons, https://commons.wikimedia.org/wiki/File:Giotto_di_bondone_e_collaboratore_napoletano,_crocifissione,_1328–1332_ca._01.JPG

16) The Crucifixion (1369/70) – Jacopo di Cione, The National Gallery, London, UK, © Wikimedia Commons, https://commons.wikimedia.org/wiki/File:Cione,_Jacopo_di_-_Crucifixion_-_National_Gallery.jpg

17) Christ Crucified between Two Thieves: The Three Crosses (1653) – Rembrandt van Rijn, Metropolitan Museum of Arts, New York, USA, © WikimediaCommons, https://commons.wikimedia.org/wiki/File:Christ_Crucified_between_the_Two_Thieves-_The_Three_Crosses_MET_DP815614.jpg

18) Crucifixion fresco (1422) – Fra Angelico, Convent of San Marco, Florence, Italy, © Wikimedia Commons, https://commons.wikimedia.org/wiki/File:Fra_Angelico_Kreuzigung_mit_Heiligen_Fresco_1441–1442_San_Marco_Florenz-1.jpg

19) Holy Door (1950) – Vico Consorti, St Peter's Basilica, Rome, Italy,© Godong/UIG / Bridgeman Images

20) Crucifixion fresco (1529) – Bernardino Luini, Church of Santa Maria degli Angeli, Lugano, Switzerland, © Wikimedia Commons, https://commons.wikimedia.org/wiki/File:Bernardino_Luini_-_Crucifixion_and_Scenes_from_the_Life_of_Christ_-_WGA13751.jpg

21) The Wales Window for Alabama (1964) – John Pett, 16th Street Baptist Church, Birmingham, Alabama, USA, © Jeffrey Isaac Greenberg / Alamy Stock Photo

22) Crucifixion – Graham Sutherland (1946). Vatican Museum, Rome, Italy, © Miscellany / Alamy Stock Photo

23) Soldiers playing dice in the Crucifixion mural (1959/60) by Jean Cocteau, Notre Dame de France, Soho, London, UK. © Photograph by Mark Thomas Jones

24) The Crucifixion of Christ (1548) – Dirck Volkertsz Coornhert, Rijksmuseum, Amsterdam, The Netherlands,©WikimediaCommons,https://commons.wikimedia.org/wiki/File:Dirck_Volkertsz._Coornhert_-_The_Crucifixion_of_Christ_-_WGA05209.jpg

25) Crucifixion: My work is done – Augustin Kolb (1869–1942), Cleveland Museum of Art, Cleveland, USA, © Wikimedia Commons, https://commons.wikimedia.org/wiki/File:Augustin_Kolb_-_Crucifixion_-_1924.253_-_Cleveland_Museum_of_Art.tif

26) Crucifixion (1420) – Master of the Rajhrad Altarpiece, National Gallery, Prague, Czech Republic, ©WikimediaCommons,https://commons.wikimedia.org/wiki/File:Uk%C5%99i%C5%BEov%C3%A1n%C3%AD_z_Nov%C3%BDch_Sad%C5%AF,_Mistr_Rajhradsk%C3%A9ho_olt%C3%A1%C5%99e,_N%C3%A1rodn%C3%AD_galerie_v_Praze.jpg

27) Crucifixion – Cretan School Icon featuring Adam's skull (17th century), State Hermitage Museum, St. Petersburg, Russia, © Wikimedia Commons, https://commons.wikimedia.org/wiki/File:CretanCrucifixion.jpg

28) Hofer altarpiece (1465) – Hans Pleydenwurff, Alte Pinakothek, Munich, Germany, ©Wikimedia Commons, https://commons.wikimedia.org/wiki/File:Hans_Pleydenwurff_-_Crucifixion_of_the_Hof_Altarpiece_-_WGA17981.jpg

29) La Piedad (1616) – Gregorio Fernandez, National Museum of Sculpture, Valladolid, Spain, © Tarker/Bridgeman Images

30) Good Thief Icon (16th Century), Rostov Kremlin, Russia © Photo: Wikipedia / Shakko, https://commons.wikimedia.org/wiki/File:Good_thief_(16th_c.,_Rostov_Kremlin).jpg

31) The Collegiate Church of the Ikon of the Mother of God Joy of All Who Sorrow, Mettingham, Suffolk, UK, © Photograph by Simon Knott

32) St. Dismas Icon Door, The Collegiate Church of the Ikon of the Mother of God Joy of All Who Sorrow, Mettingham, Suffolk, UK, © Photograph by Simon Knott

33) Voroneţ Monastery, © Church of St George, Voronet Monastery, Bukovina, Romania/Bridgeman Images

34) The Penitent Thief (1918) – Francis Derwent Wood, © Lady Lever Art Gallery, National Museums Liverpool, UK/Bridgeman Images

35) Ivory carving of the Crucifixion (Tenth Century) – Walters Art Museum, Baltimore, USA, ©Wikimedia Commons, https://commons.wikimedia.org/wiki/File:Byzantine_-_Crucifixion_-_Walters_7165.jpg

36) The Good Thief featured carrying his cross in a Twelfth century mosaic of the Last Judgement in the Basilica di Santa Maria Assunta, Torcello, Italy, ©Wikimedia Commons, https://commons.wikimedia.org/wiki/File:Unknown_artist_-_Last_Judgment_(detail)_-_WGA16284.jpg

37) The Crucifixion (circa 1310) – Duccio di Buoninsegna, Manchester Art Gallery, UK, ©Wikimedia Commons, https://commons.wikimedia.org/wiki/File:Duccio_di_Buoninsegna_-_Crucifixion_-_WGA06721.jpg

38) Le bon larron (The Good Thief) Dismas (14th century) – Strasbourg Cathedral, France, ©Wikimedia Commons,https://commons.wikimedia.org/wiki/File:Stra%C3%9Fburger_M%C3%B-Cnster,_Glasmalerei,_III-13.jpg

39) The Good Thief St. Dismas (circa 1455) – Unknown Spanish Master, National Gallery of Denmark, Copenhagen, ©Wikimedia Commons, https://commons.wikimedia.org/wiki/File:Ubekendt_spansk_mester_-_The_Good_Thief_(Saint_Dismas)_-_KMS8561_-_Statens_Museum_for_Kunst.jpg

40) The Crucifixion with the Virgin and Saint John the Evangelist Mourning (circa 1460) – Rogier van der Weyden, Philadelphia Museum of Art, Philadelphia, USA, ©Wikimedia Commons https://commons.wikimedia.org/wiki/File:Rogier_van_der_Weyden,_Netherlandish_(active_Tournai_and_Brussels)_-_The_Crucifixion,_with_the_Virgin_and_Saint_John_the_Evangelist_Mourning_-_Google_Art_Project.jpg

41) Crucifixion/Antwerpen Crucifixion (1475) – Antonello de Messina, Royal Museum of Fine Arts, Antwerp, Belgium. ©Wikimedia Commons, https://commons.wikimedia.org/wiki/File:Antonello_da_Messina_026.jpg

42) Passion of Christ fresco (circa 1491), Giovanni Canavesio, Notre Dame de Fontaine Chapelle, La Brigue, France, ©Wikimedia Commons, https://commons.wikimedia.org/wiki/File:-La_Brigue_-_Chapelle_Notre-Dame-des-Fontaines_-_Nef_-_Fresques_de_la_Passion_du_Christ_-16.JPG

43) Passion of Christ fresco (circa 1491) featuring the Harrowing of Hell, Giovanni Canavesio, Notre Dame de Fontaine Chapelle, La Brigue, France, ©Wikimedia Commons, https://commons.wikimedia.org/wiki/File:La_Brigue_-_Chapelle_Notre-Dame-des-Fontaines_-_Nef_-_Fresques_de_la_Passion_du_Christ_-18.JPG

44) St Dismas stained glass (circa 1539) – Church of Saint-Yves, La Roche-Maurice, Brittany, France, ©Wikimedia Commons, https://commons.wikimedia.org/wiki/File:La_Roche-Maurice_(29)_%C3%89glise_Saint-Yves_Ma%C3%AEtresse-vitre_019.JPG

45) Detail of Dismas – The Good Thief in a Sixteenth Century stained glass window located in the Chapel of St. Martin in the Catholic Church of Saint Pierre, Dreux, The Loire Valley, France. ©Wikimedia Commons, Photograph by G. Freihalter, https://upload.wikimedia.org/wikipedia/commons/a/a2/Dreux_Saint-Pierre_Christ_en_Croix_349.JPG

46) The Crucifixion of Christ (Sixteenth Century) – Hans Speckaert, Metroplitan Museum of Art, New York, USA, ©Wikimedia Commons, https://commons.wikimedia.org/wiki/File:Hans_Speckaert_-_The_Crucifixion_of_Christ.jpg

47) Dimas, the Good Thief, from the Sixth Anguish of the Virgin Mary by Gregorio Fernández (circa 1616), National Museum of Sculpture, Valladolid, Spain, ©Wikimedia Commons, https://commons.wikimedia.org/wiki/File:Dimas,_el_Buen_Ladr%C3%B3n_(Paso_de_la_Sexta_Angustia).JPG

48) The Crucifixion (1711) Ionnis Moskos, Digitized Archive of the Hellenic Institute of Venice. The Wise Robber is turned towards Christ and saying; "Remember me, Lord in your Kingdom.", ©Wikimedia Commons, https://commons.wikimedia.org/wiki/File:Crucifixion_by_I.Moskos_(1711).jpg

49) Altar painting of der Gute Schächer (the Good Thief) by Joseph Karpf (1733) in the Catholic Church of the Visitation of the Virgin Mary, Gottmannshofen, Bavaria, Germany. ©Wikimedia Commons, Photograph by G. Freihalter, https://commons.wikimedia.org/wiki/File:Gottmanshofen_Mari%C3%A4_Heimsuchung_Altarauszug_562.JPG

50) Statue of St. Dismas (1750) on a bridge in Březnice, Příbram district, Czech Republic, ©Wikimedia Commons, https://commons.wikimedia.org/wiki/File:Breznice_PB_CZ_St_Dismas_638.jpg

51) Church of Saint Dismas in the village of Dříteň, České Budějovice District, Czech Republic, ©Wikimedia Commons, https://commons.wikimedia.org/wiki/File:D%C5%99%C3%ADte%C5%88_10a.jpg

52) Statue of San Dimas in the Basílica de Nuestra Señora de Zapopan (Basilica of Our Lady of Zapopan), Jalisco, Mexico, ©Wikimedia Commons, https://commons.wikimedia.org/wiki/File:Bas%C3%ADlica_de_Nuestra_Se%C3%B1ora_de_Zapopan_(Jalisco,_Mexico)_-_statue,_St._Dismas.jpg

53) Wall painting in Ura Kidane Mihret, an Ethiopian Orthodox Church on the Zege Peninsula, on the southern shores of Lake Tana, Ethiopia, ©Wikimedia Commons, Photograph by Adam Jones, https://commons.wikimedia.org/wiki/File:Crucifixion_Scene_-_Ura_Kidane_Mihret_(Church)_-_Zege_Peninsula_-_Near_Bahir_Dar_-_Ethiopia_(8679575901).jpg

54) Crucifixion scene painted on the façade of the I Yesus Church, Axum (Aksum), Tigray Region, Ethiopia, ©Wikimedia Commons, Photograph by Adam Jones, https://commons.wikimedia.org/wiki/File:Crucifixion_Scene_on_Facade_of_I_Yesus_Church_-_Axum_(Aksum)_-_Ethiopia_(8701135115).jpg

55) The Crucifixion by the Romans (1887) – Vasily Vereshchagin, Private Collection, ©Wikimedia Commons, https://commons.wikimedia.org/wiki/File:Crucifixion_by_the_Romans_(Vasily_Vereshchagin_-_1887).jpg

56) Crucifixion with Darkened Sun (1907) – Egon Schiele, ©Wikimedia Commons https://commons.wikimedia.org/wiki/File:Schiel01.jpg

57) Calvary (1926) – Alfred Frank Hardiman, Old St. Paul's Church, Edinburgh, UK, ©Wikimedia Commons, https://commons.wikimedia.org/wiki/File:Hardiman_calvary_1926.jpg

58) Christ Head (1952) – Alexis Preller, Iziko South African National Gallery, Cape Town, South Africa, ©Wikimedia Commons, https://commons.wikimedia.org/wiki/File:Iziko_sang_Christ_Head.jpg

59) Chapel of St. Dismas, Zagreb, Croatia, © Photo by Anamaria Mejia / Alamy Stock Photo

60) St. Dismas on one of the deacon's doors, St. Nicholas Orthodox Church, Fletcher, North Carolina, USA, © Photograph by Mary-Jo Dukas

DISMAS

THE PENITENT THIEF
AN INTRODUCTION

Mark Thomas Jones

CITADELLE

To the memory of the late
Monsignor Augustine Hoey obl. OSB
(1915–2017).
Fr. Augustine was one of those beacons of faith
who illuminated my Christian path
and helped me to realise that acceptance
must start from within.

One of the great works of Nineteenth century English Literature is Charles Dicken's historical novel *A Tale of Two Cities* (1859) set against the background of the French Revolution. As the story reaches its denouement Sydney Carton, one of the central characters, whilst en route to the guillotine has his final thoughts verbalised by Dickens as follows: *"It is a far, far better thing that I do, that I have ever done; it is a far, far better rest that I go to than I have ever known."* These words are worth reflecting upon and are germane to the story and significance of The Penitent Thief, otherwise known as Dismas/St. Dismas.

Just as late Eighteenth-century France was a turbulent age; First century Judaea was no stranger to agitation and violence. Much of the known world was ruled from Rome, and whilst the Roman Empire prided itself on what it saw as the *Pax Romana* the reality for many lands and territories was that they were subject to alien and unforgiving Roman Law. For the Jews and other subject peoples, the rule and justice they experienced from the Romans amounted to an imperial tyranny that is best summed up as their being under *"the heel of insolent might"*[1].

Jesus of Nazareth was born during the reign of the Roman Emperor Augustus (27BC–14AD) and put to death by crucifixion in the time of Emperor Tiberius (14–37AD). The events that centre upon this crucifixion involved a whole host of historical figures including Pontius Pilate, the Governor of the Roman Province of Judaea, Herod Antipas, the tetrarch of Galilee and Peraea, and Caiaphas, a Jewish high priest who presided over the Sanhedrin trial of Jesus. The execution of Jesus along with two thieves at Golgotha (a word derived from the Aramaic

---

1   A phrase coined by Philip Goodrich, the Bishop of Worcester and first used in a Holy Week homily at St. Matthias Church, Malvern Link, Worcestershire, England in April 1987. The author was present at this occasion.

for 'skull' – hence 'the place of the skull'[2] as referred to in Matthew 27:33) elucidates something of the barbarism of the time, as well as the fulfilment of what had been foretold in the Old Testament. The behaviour of the two criminals is worthy of analysis, especially as one, The Penitent Thief, in a Cartonesque way redeemed himself in his dying hours and thus achieved a sublime rest with Jesus Christ in Paradise.

WHY WAS JESUS CRUCIFIED?

To Christians of differing denominations[3] the events of Holy Week that culminated in Jesus's death and resurrection provide ample scope to highlight human frailty and malevolence. In Jesus here was a figure who on what is commemorated as Palm Sunday, was welcomed into Jerusalem and acclaimed as a saviour and liberator by some and yet within a matter of days was betrayed, arrested, interrogated, 'tried'[4], sentenced, scourged, mocked and put to death. From a theological perspective it could be argued that the death of Jesus was all part of God's Divine Plan, for as a result of his martyrdom by crucifixion and death – the death and resurrection of the Son of God – mankind's relationship with God would be restored. This supreme act of Atonement was to be central to Christian belief, and the understanding of Jesus's act of self-sacrifice, one that reconciles mankind with God.

---

2 Meaning of Golgotha – Available at: www.biblestudytools.com/dictionary/golgotha/ [Accessed 11 March 2020]

3 The Orthodox Church sees itself as pre-denominational rather than denominational.

4 Jesus was tried by the Sanhedrin, Pontius Pilate, and Herod Antipas. The following paper makes interesting reading in this regard: Tyson, J. (1959). The Lukan Version of the Trial of Jesus. *Novum Testamentum*, 3(4), pp. 249–258.

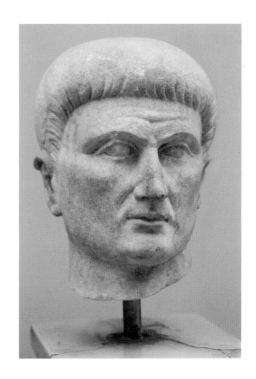

1 Sculptured head of the Emperor Tiberius – 1st century AD – Archaeological Museum of Istanbul, Turkey. Tiberius was the Roman Emperor at the time of the Crucifixion.

But why was Jesus crucified in 33AD?[5] To some he was a subversive and a troublemaker. His views were deemed socially and religiously unorthodox. Here was a man who mixed with those on the margins of society, or with people who were viewed as outcasts or unclean. Much of what Jesus said and did was looked upon, especially by conservative elements in the Jewish religious establishment, as being blasphemous[6] and anti-authoritarian. Jesus of Nazareth was viewed with intense suspicion in some quarters and seen as dangerous and a clear threat. The religious powers that be were eager to denounce him to the Roman authorities and wanted him to be put to death. As for the Romans they were wary of those that might incite social unrest, or who could

---

5 It is important to note that scholars are still at variance as to the precise year in which Jesus was crucified, equally debate continues as to the length of his ministry. The following paper provides some food for thought: Zeitlin, S. (1965). The Duration of Jesus' Ministry. *The Jewish Quarterly Review, 55*(3), 181–200.

6 Tibor Horvath explores this matter extensively in the following paper: Horvath, T. (1969). Why was Jesus Brought to Pilate? *Novum Testamentum, 11*(3), pp. 174–184.

become a focal point for any movement that would challenge their rule and the status quo. Yet it became clear from Jesus's encounters with and the utterances and behaviour of the Roman Governor of Judaea that he was viewed as somewhat of an enigma, albeit one who elicited strong reactions from the Jewish religious authorities.

Whilst some sought to portray Jesus as some form of revolutionary, intent on overthrowing the Establishment and thus potentially an enemy of Rome, *ergo* Emperor Tiberius, events as recounted in the New Testament make clear that it was not for political offences that he was executed, but for religious ones that were contrary to Jewish Law. It was Jesus's supposed blasphemy that was the driving force behind the campaign by some to convince Pontius Pilate that Jesus should be killed.

The nature of power in an empire such as that of Rome meant that individuals like Pontius Pilate were often ambitious and venal characters.[7] That said, being Governor of the Province of Judaea was no mere sinecure. Judaea was viewed as a highly truculent province, one where the monotheistic inhabitants were as likely to be at odds with their own local rulers as they were their Roman masters. In respect of the fate of Jesus of Nazareth, Pontius Pilate found himself in an invidious position, one which meant he faced a moral dilemma. Provincial governors in the Roman Empire had a range of powers at their disposal, one of which was that of *jus gladii* (the right of the sword) – the executory power of the law, the power of life and death.[8] The Gospel accounts make clear that Pilate was ill at ease with the prospect of sending Jesus to his death, whilst at the same time having

---

7   McGing, B. (1991). Pontius Pilate and the Sources. *The Catholic Biblical Quarterly, 53*(3), pp. 416–438.

8   Garnsey, P. (1968). The Criminal Jurisdiction of Governors. *The Journal of Roman Studies, 58*, pp. 51–59

to avoid enflaming a potentially volatile situation. The fact that the population of Jerusalem was swollen with visitors for the Jewish Feast of Passover (the Feast of Unleavened Bread) added to the dynamic and made him and other Romans present acutely aware of the potential for a riot, borne in part out of anti-Roman sentiment. Crowds could easily become agitated and there might be the need to deploy military detachments that would be likely to result in multiple casualties and deaths. Even the Jewish High Priests and the Elders were sensitive about acting against Jesus during the Passover; *"lest there be a tumult among the people."* (Matthew 26:5). Pontius Pilate could be said to have been in a Catch-22 situation, for he was being exhorted to execute a man whom he appeared to believe to be innocent, or face the danger of civil insurrection and the political fallout resulting from brutally suppressing such a disturbance. Whatever the Roman Governor's personal faults, it is possible to empathise with his predicament. In respect of what was to happen to Jesus of Nazareth, from the perspective of the Old Testament the die was cast.

In the Gospels it is evident that Pontius Pilate was not convinced of Jesus's guilt, certainly not in respect of anything warranting capital punishment. There is clear evidence of Pilate's attempts at diplomatic and moral funambulism, something that has often been overlooked with the passage of time; in part this is due to the enormity of the crime that Christians believe was perpetrated against their Messiah.[9] That said, he was also mindful of the sensitivities around religious matters, conscious that with the monotheistic Jews issues appertaining to religion were often far more dogmatic than they might be among polytheistic cultures. The New Testament makes it apparent that

---

9   This later led to the notion of the Jewish Deicide, a myopic and dangerous idea that in some quarters has fostered rabid anti-semitism, persecution and genocide.

2   *Christ Carrying the Cross*
(1500–1535) – By a follower of
Hieronymous Bosch, Museum of
Fine Arts, Ghent, Belgium. Having
to carry the instrument of their
execution often through hostile
crowds was deemed all part
of the punishment for those
condemned to death.

3   *Via Dolorosa sign*,
Jersusalem, Israel – Photograph by
Paul Arps. The sign is in Hebrew,
Arabic and Latin and translates as
The Way of Sorrow. This is the
route which Jesus is believed to
have taken to his crucifixion.

Pilate spoke to Jesus on several occasions and that; *"Pilate sought to release him, but the Jews cried out, "If you release this man, you are not Caesar's friend;"* (John 19:12). The Roman Governor aware of certain irregularities and sensing the doing of an injustice endeavoured to find a way out of having to execute Jesus. It was customary during the Feast of the Passover for the Roman Governor to pardon and release a prisoner; he hoped that this might be an opportunity to extricate himself and the Nazarene, who had been dubbed the King of the Jews, from this difficult situation. *"And the crowd came up and began to ask Pilate to do as he was wont to do for them. And he answered them, 'Do you want me to release for you the King of the Jews?' For he perceived that it was out of envy that the chief priests had delivered him up. But the chief priests stirred up the crowd to have him release for them Barab'bas instead. And Pilate again said to them, 'then what shall I do with the man whom you call the King of the Jews?' And they cried out again, 'Crucify him'."* (Mark 15:8–14) The Gospel according to Matthew goes on to recount how the Roman Governor endeavoured to try and absolve himself of any guilt; *"So when Pilate saw that he was gaining nothing, but rather that a riot was beginning, he took water and washed his hands before the crowd, saying, 'I am innocent of this man's blood, see to it yourselves.' And all the people answered, 'His blood be on us and our children!' Then he released for them Barab'bas, and having scourged Jesus, delivered him to be crucified."*. (Matthew 27: 24–26)

WHAT WAS CRUCIFIXION?

In the Ancient World executions were often brutal, and in the case of crucifixion designed to be both degrading and drawn-out. Crucifixion was carried out on various malefactors: these might be slaves who had displeased or done harm to their owners, to disgraced soldiers, violent criminals, highway robbers or those labelled as enemies of the state. Adriano Prosperi states that; *"The bifurcated tree was the symbol and the instrument of an ignominious and painful death."*[10] The cross generally believed to have been used in crucifixion had a vertical beam sticking above the *patibulum* (horizontal or crossbeam) and was known as a *crux immissa* or *crux capitata*; upon subsequently being adopted as a Christian symbol it became known as the Latin cross. A cross sometimes featured a *suppedaneum*, which was a piece of wood that served as a foot-support, and possibly an *eculus*[11] which acted as a crotch-support for those being crucified. It is important to appreciate that some historians and indeed early Fathers of the Church have been of the view that Jesus and the two criminals were crucified using a T-shaped[12] cross. Other forms of cross were used in crucifixions.[13] A standard crucifixion, if ever there was such a thing, involved those to be put to death being nailed to the cross with arms outstretched, using four nails, two for the hands and two for the feet.

Crucifixion was a very public form of execution designed to humiliate the victim and serve as an object lesson to others. Whilst not invented by the Romans, it was a frequent feature of their repertoire of retribution against those they wished to feel the full force of the

---

10 Prosperi, A. (2018) *Justice Blindfolded: The Historical Course of an Image*, Brill, Leiden. pp. 75–76

11 Hewitt, J. (1932). The Use of Nails in the Crucifixion. *The Harvard Theological Review, 25*(1), pp. 29–45.

12 A T-shaped cross is often known as a Tau Cross, so called because it is shaped like the Greek letter *tau* when in its upper-case. In respect of its use in execution it is sometimes called the *crux commisa*. Llewellyn Jewiitt notes that it can also go by the name *crux ansata* or the Cross of St. Antony. Jewitt, L. (1875). The Cross Tau, as an Emblem and in Art. *The Art Journal (1875–1887), 1*, new series, pp. 301–304. Tim Healey's insight on this subject is of merit – Healey, T. (1977). The Symbolism of the Cross in Sacred and Secular Art. *Leonardo, 10*(4), pp. 289–294.

13 These include *crux simplex*, which was essentially an upright stake; a *furca*, a Y-shaped cross and the *crux decussata*, which was X-shaped.

20

might and displeasure of Rome. Those sentenced to be crucified were stripped naked, scourged, and forced to carry their cross to the place of execution. Once nailed to the wooden cross, it was then hoisted upright and guarded by soldiers.

"Death, usually after 6 hours–4 days, was due to multifactorial pathology: after-effects of compulsory scourging and maiming, haemorrhage and dehydration causing hypovolemic shock and pain, but the most important factor was progressive asphyxia caused by impairment of respiratory movement. Resultant anoxaemia exaggerated hypovolemic shock. Death was probably commonly precipitated by cardiac arrest, caused by vasovagal reflexes, initiated inter alia by severe anoxaemia, severe pain, body blows and breaking of the large bones. The attending Roman guards could only leave the site after the victim had died, and were known to precipitate death by means of deliberate fracturing of the tibia and/or fibula, spear stab wounds into the heart, sharp blows to the front of the chest, or a smoking fire built at the foot of the cross to asphyxiate the victim."[14]

Often to add to the horror and effectiveness of the punishment bodies were not allowed to be taken down to have a decent burial and were left to rot and be a gruesome warning to others. By so doing many believed that those who had ordered the execution were able to extend the reach of their retribution into the afterlife.

WHAT IS KNOWN ABOUT THE PENITENT THIEF?

Felons are very rarely the subject of scholarship, principally as in the Roman Empire life was viewed as cheap and people expendable. Those on the margins of society or who lived a renegade existence rarely featured in official records, especially as vengeful powers often

---

14 Quoted from the Abstract of the following academic paper: Cilliers, L. & Retief, F.P (2003). The history and pathology of crucifixion. *South African Medical Journal* 93 (12), pp. 938–41.

4 *The Raising of the Cross* (1524) – Jörg Breu the Elder, Museum of Fine Arts, Budapest, Hungary. This painting clearly shows some of the paraphernalia required to carry out a crucifixion.

wanted to obliterate the memory of those who had incurred their displeasure. The person known as the Good, Penitent or Wise Thief, or to some Dismas/St. Dismas, has a decidedly shadowy past; it is only at his execution and death that he emerges as a key figure in the Passion of Christ. Whilst both he and his fellow criminal are given prominence when they are crucified either side of Jesus, there is nothing that tells what they had done to warrant such a violent death. The term 'thief' is routinely used, although some including Flavius Josephus (37–100 AD), the Roman-Jewish historian, have posited that Dismas was an insurgent, possibly a Zealot, hence the gravity of the sentence. Admirers of the writing of Mikhail Bulgakov (1891–1940), specifically *The Master and Margarita,* will be firmly convinced that Dismas was sentenced to death for helping instigate a rebellion against Caesar, an opinion that might well chime with some scholars. Others have speculated whether Dismas was guilty of fratricide among other crimes; the truth is that whatever tradition says, we are still largely in the dark.

The names of the two thieves is largely derived from an apocryphal gospel known generally as the *Gospel of Nicodemus*.[15] Biblical scholars believe that this document dates from the mid-4th century AD, although it has earlier elements to it, and thus is probably by multiple authors. From it the thieves are identified as Dysmas (The Penitent Thief) and Gestas (The Impenitent Thief). Through the ages there have been variations on the names with Dismas, Dimas or Demas being used for the one and Cismas, Gestas, Gesmas or Testas being used for the other. The names of the two thieves as Dismas and Gestas became established after being included in a Fourteenth century work

---

15 Sometimes known as the *Acts of Pilate.*

Legends of the Saints by Petrus de Natalibus. The etymology of the name Dismas is open to debate, with some believing that it is derived from the Greek word δυσμη *dysme*, meaning *"sunset"*;[16] this would be argued to be fitting as it was at the sunset of his life that Dismas trusted in God's Mercy. This possible explanation is given added credence by the fact that early Syrian representations of the Crucifixion featured a sun and moon over the thieves' heads, for instance in the *Syriac Rabbula Gospels*,[17] the dramatic coloration usually connoted a sunset; the setting of the sun and the subsequent sunrise being a traditional sign of a new day and fresh hope, hope being viewed as something to be found in the penitent and those acknowledging Jesus Christ as Saviour. Some scholars have advanced the idea that the Good Thief's name means *"death"*,[18] with his death and recognition of the sovereignty of Christ being his route to Salvation. As to his precise origins, and whether he was Jew or Gentile, there has been some speculation. In Israel there is a strategic hilltop location called Latrun overlooking the Jerusalem to Tel Aviv road, one theory put forward by toponymists is that this name is derived from the Latin *domus boni Latronis* (The House of the Good Thief); whether Dismas was born locally or possibly lived in the vicinity remains a matter of conjecture. Some in the past were convinced that Dismas was an Egyptian,[19] but nothing exists that can prove for certain where he hailed from. Had he been an Egyptian, and

16 Behind the Name – Dismas – Available at: www.behindthename.com/name/dismas/comments [Accessed 3 February 2020]

17 Savage, J. (2018) *The Iconography of Darkness at the Crucifixion* – The Index of Medieval Art – https://ima.princeton.edu/2018/04/04/the-iconography-of-crucifixion-darkness/ [Accessed 29 March 2020]

18 A Letter to "The Good Thief" on Good Friday – Available at: www.americamagazine.org/content/all-things/letter-good-thief-good-friday [Accessed 7 February 2020]

19 Gaume, J. & Lisle, M. de (tr.) (2003), *Life of the Good Thief*. Loreto Publications, Fitzwilliam, p. 21

a likely polytheist, his acknowledgement of Christ on the Cross would have been even more of a revelation.

Prominent figures of the Early Christian Church such as Cyprian of Carthage (circa 200–258 AD)[20], St. John Chrysostom (circa 347–407 AD) and St. Augustine of Hippo (354–430 AD) reflected on Dismas and his death, with the former describing him as having been a murderer. St. Cyril of Alexandria (378–444 AD), Patriach of Alexandria and eminent theologian, in *On the Dread of Judgment* describes the Good Thief at the Crucifixion as being *"a fellow traveller"* with Jesus.[21] Most of what has come down to us about Dismas's early life is via legendary lore and thus it needs to be treated with a healthy degree of circumspection. All churches focus on the ultimate destination, with the Orthodox Church calling the thief that turned to Christ the Wise Thief in view of his discernment and faith demonstrated on the cross. In the apocryphal *Syriac Infancy Gospels* (also known as the *Arabic Infancy Gospels*)[22] believed to date from the fifth or sixth centuries AD there is reference to two thieves, Titus and Dumachus, with the former (The Good Thief) preventing the latter (The Bad Thief) and possibly other associates from doing harm to the Holy Family during their Flight to Egypt[23]. This same account of Titus and Dumachus appears in the *Book of the Bee*, a historical theological compilation by Solomon of Akhlat, a Syrian Bishop of the Church of the East (Nestorian Church) written circa 1222. These narratives echo much of what was

---

20 Daigneault, A. (2005) *The Good Thief*, Xulon Press, Maitland, p. 41.

21 Doval, A. (2001) *Cyril of Jerusalem, Mystagogue*, The Catholic University of America Press, Washington DC.

22 Arabic Infancy Gospel – NASCALL – Available at: www.nasscal.com/e-clavis-christian-apocrypha/arabic-infancy-gospel/ [Accessed 17 April 2020]

23 The Holy Family refers to Jesus, Mary, and Joseph, with the Flight into Egypt being viewed as the second of the Seven Sorrows of Mary.

described elsewhere, along with the contrast that emerges in the narrative of the Passion of Christ. Dismas makes an appearance in the writing of St. Anselm of Canterbury (1033–1109) where in an account of Jesus's childhood Anselm describes how during the Holy Family's Flight to Egypt[24] Dismas and his fellow brigands spotted the travellers and planned to waylay and rob them. As they drew close-by he was so struck by the sanctity and grace that shone on the countenance of the infant Jesus that Dismas prevailed upon (some say bribed) his fellow brigands to refrain from harming the travellers. Later versions of this narrative claim that he gave shelter and assistance to the Holy Family and that Mary promised that he would be blessed later in life for his act of charity. The Fourteenth century Liége chronicler Jean d'Outremeuse (1338–1400) provides in *Ly Myreur des Histors* (The Mirror of Histories) some interesting additional detail concerning this supposed encounter during the Flight to Egypt. Whilst there is limited evidence in Scripture to support this story, indeed it is not found in the Canonical Gospels,[25] in various Christian traditions it has gained a general credence. Often it is the case that chroniclers, historians and theologians in the Middle Ages drew much of their inspiration from the Biblical apocrypha. In the words of the eminent Belgian philologist Jacques Poucet; *"The Apocrypha has filled the void left by the canonical texts."*[26] Nothing else is known of Dismas until his appearance in the Passion narrative.

---

24 St. Dismas by Plinio Corrêa de Oliveira – Available at: www.traditioninaction.org/SOD/j238sd_Dismas_03_12.html [Accessed 20 February 2020]
25 Matthew (2:13–23) records the Holy Family's Flight to Egypt, but there is no mention of any encounters with brigands.
26 Jacques Poucet 'The Flight of the Holy Family into Egypt with Jean d'Outremeuse', FEC (Folia Electronica Classica, Issue 28, 2014) Available at: http://bcs.fltr.ucl.ac.be/FE/28/Egypt_MM/Egyptien/Juxta.htm [Accessed 1 May 2020]

5 *Crucifixion of Christ/Wilten Crucifixion* (1435) – Unknown Tyrolean Painter, Upper Belvedere, Vienna, Austria. Probably originally from All Saints Church, Hart near Innsbruck in the Tyrol. Painted on spruce wood and featuring a T-shaped or Tau cross.

In writing from the medieval period Dismas is given a degree of prominence for the example that he provides of someone who acknowledges his own sinfulness and as a result gains last-minute salvation. A key source from the mid-Thirteenth Century that gained wide exposure during the Middle Ages is Jacobus de Voragine's *Golden Legend*.[27] Furthermore, works such as *Piers Plowman* by William Langland (1332–1386) feature characters that cling to the story of Dismas's part in the Crucifixion as one of hope for sinners. The Good Thief also features in *Arts Moriendi* (The Art of Dying)[28] two Latin texts that are believed to have been written in southern Germany during the early part of the Fifteenth century. Alexander Gabrovsky observes that; *"It is common in medieval artwork and literature to stress the visual and emotional likeness of the crucified Dismas to Christ...".*[29] Art from the Middle Ages occasionally features the Good Thief accompanying Jesus in the Harrowing of Hell, an event in which Jesus descends triumphantly into Hell during the period between his Crucifixion and Ascension. This is commemorated in the Apostle's Creed and is the time when Jesus brought salvation to all the righteous who had died since the dawn of time. Some theologians and Biblical scholars continue to debate the timings and events that happened after the Crucifixion, yet for all of this, it is in the Gospels that the most understanding of the Penitent Thief is to be found.

27 Le Goff, J. (2014) *In Search of Sacred Time*, Princeton University Press, Princeton, p.103.
28 Art Through Time – A Page from the *Arts Moriendi* – Available at: www.learner.org/series/art-through-time-a-global-view/death/a-page-from-the-ars-moriendi/ [Accessed 2 April 2020]
29 Gobrovsky, A. (2011) The Good, the Bad, and the Penitent Thief: Langlandian Extremes, and the Edge of Salvation, and the Problem of Trajan and Dismas in *Piers Plowman, Marginalia*, 12 p. 3.

DISMAS AND THE CANONICAL GOSPELS

The Gospels of Matthew, Mark, Luke and John all mention that Jesus was crucified with two others, with Jesus in the middle (Matthew 27:38; Mark 15:27; Luke 23:33 and John 19:18), with only John's Gospel not mentioning the fact that the other two were criminals. Jesus being crucified between two thieves could be seen as a direct fulfilment of the Prophesy in The Book of Isaiah: *"and was numbered with the transgressors; yet he bore the sin of many, and made intercession for the transgressors."* (Isaiah 53:12). The first three Gospels are particularly illuminating in respect of the role of the thieves, although at no point are the criminals named. In the following pericope Matthew recounts how Jesus had been singled out for ridicule:

"Then the soldiers of the governor took Jesus into the praetorium, and they gathered the whole battalion before him. And they stripped him and put a scarlet robe upon him, and plaiting a crown of thorns they put it on his head and put a reed in his right hand. And kneeling before him they mocked him, saying 'Hail, King of the Jews!' and they spat upon him, and took the reed and struck him on the head. And when they had mocked him, they stripped him of the robe, and put his own clothes on him and led him away to crucify him." (Matthew 27:27–31).

Once nailed to the cross and hoisted up between the two thieves Jesus was jeered at and derided by the spectators; *"And the robbers who were crucified with him also reviled him in the same way."* (Matthew 27:44). Mark's Gospel also confirms that both the thieves reviled Jesus (Mark 15:32). Yet it is to Luke's Gospel that we must turn for the evidence of the Penitent Thief.

"One of the criminals who were hanged railed at him (Jesus), saying, 'Are you not the Christ? Save yourself and us!' But the other rebuked him, saying, 'do you not fear God, since you are under the same sentence of condemnation?

And we indeed justly; for we are receiving the due reward of our deeds; but this man has done nothing wrong.' And he said, 'Jesus, remember me when you come in your kingly power.' And he said to him, 'Truly, I say to you, today you will be with me in Paradise.' "(Luke 23:39–43).[30]

The Penitent Thief by defending Jesus not only does a good deed, he speaks the truth. Abbé Leonard Joseph Marie Cros S. J.[31] writes of the Good Thief's *"pious audacity"*[32] in his public witness of the innocence of Jesus. Dismas's courage on the cross could be viewed as a form of expiation for his life of sin. Moreover, such an act stands in marked contrast with those who melted away when Jesus was betrayed by Judas Iscariot and arrested, and then denied by Simon Peter. Dismas even at the time of his degradation and execution finds it within himself not only to acknowledge the innocence of Jesus Christ, but also through his declaration of faith clearly connotes his acceptance of Christ not only as a king, but one who will triumph over death. In his words it is evident that the Penitent Thief believes in the power of Jesus, not to save his mortal self *per se*, but to save his soul. It is interesting that he does not ask to be in Paradise, but merely to be remembered. What can we learn from this in respect of the importance of humility?

When the Penitent Thief makes his humble request to Jesus to *"remember me"* (Luke 23:42) it is possible to appreciate that here are words with a deep significance, not only for Dismas, but for the whole of mankind. In this context remembrance is so much more than the act of recollection, it is rich with associations throughout Judeo-Christian worship. The Crucifixion took place at the time of the gathering for the

---

30 New Testament scholars continue to debate the differences in the accounts and whether one or more of the criminals reviled Jesus.

31 S.J. is the abbreviation for the Society of Jesus, a religious order of the Catholic Church. Members of that order are known as Jesuits.

32 Cros, L. (1870) *Le Bon Larron*, Régnault, Toulouse, p. 28.

Feast of the Passover, an occasion with profound meaning, when the Jews remembered their time of slavery in Egypt and how God had not forgotten His chosen people. Exodus 12:14 embodies how the Passover became an act of rememberance and of worship: *"This day shall be for you a memorial day, and you shall keep it as a feast to the LORD; throughout your generations you shall observe it as an ordinance forever."* Jesus in the Last Supper shared a Passover meal with his disciples, an act commemorated and recalled in the Christian rite of the Eucharist (the Mass or Holy Communion). When we celebrate the Eucharist[33] we not only remember Jesus's sacrifice, but its significance, that the Eucharist reaffirms belief in his act of Atonement for all mankind. Sacerdotal duties and ritual ensure that this act of remembrance has a reverence and meaning far beyond recall of an event recorded in the New Testament. By participating in the Eucharist, we reaffirm our belief, recommit to God, and remember that Jesus Christ died for us, each, and every one of us. For it is in the Eucharist that the mystery of the Cross becomes a reality.

When Dismas made his request to Jesus on the Cross there is the added dimension of the fact that the omniscience of God meant that Dismas's transgressions, and there were many, were known and remembered, a point relevant to us all. The Bible is replete with requests, instructions and exhortations to remember; in the Good Thief's case the request is made with courage and humility, his is a mental and spiritual obeisance before the Son of Man, something which in view of his past makes the definitive response that he receives both remarkable and heartening. Dismas through his supplication on the cross serves as a reminder of the significance of meekness and of the acknowledgement and abnegation of sin. It is worth remembering

---

33 The Eucharist is considered a sacrament in most churches, and an ordinance in others.

the words of Jesus in John 6:40 *"For this is the will of my Father, that every one who sees the Son and believes in him should have eternal life; and I will raise him up at the last day."* Dismas had been lost, but through Jesus Christ he was both found and saved.

THE ICONOGRAPHY OF THE CRUCIFIXION

The Crucifixion on what is now marked as Good Friday is replete with powerful imagery and symbolism. With the place of execution being on the outskirts of Jerusalem it was easily accessible for those who wanted to watch this grisly spectacle. Golgotha, sometimes known as Calvary (both words referring to the skull, more particularly the cranium – the skull-pan of the head) is believed to have been located a relatively short distance from the Jewish Temple. As an event the Crucifixion is the apotheosis of the New Testament and warrants close and careful analysis. From the four Canonical Gospels it is possible to work out some of the people who were present at the execution: Mary (mother of Jesus), Mary Magdalene[34], Joseph of Arimathea, Nicodemus, Salome (often identified as the wife of Zebedee), Mary of Clopas, Simon of Cyrene and a Disciple (historically believed to have been John, although this remains a matter of debate). Furthermore, it is possible to infer that the following were present: A Roman Centurion (possibly called Longinus)[35] along with Caiaphas and Annas, both High Priests. Four soldiers were assigned to carry out the execution, and of course

---

34 Mary Magdalene often appears *sub cruce* dressed in red with flowing hair. A fascinating read on this subject is: Bohde, D. (2019). Mary Magdalene at the Foot of the Cross: Iconography and the Semantics of Place. *Mitteilungen Des Kunsthistorischen Institutes in Florenz, 61*(1), pp.3–44.

35 J. Ramsey Michaels asserts that the name of Longinus made its first appearance in the pseudo-*Gospel of Nicodemus*. Michaels, J. (1967). The Centurion's Confession and the Spear Thrust. *The Catholic Biblical Quarterly, 29*(1), pp.102–109.

there were the three individuals to be put to death: Jesus of Nazareth and the two unnamed thieves. Jerusalem was exceptionally busy with visitors present for the Passover and so it is likely that quite a crowd of spectators would have gathered. Whilst some of those watching would have been full of vengeful satisfaction at the fact that Jesus was to be executed, others present were distraught at what was taking place. Anyone who has seen the 1964 film *Il vangelo secondo Matteo* (The Gospel According to St. Matthew)[36] by the Italian director Pier Paolo Pasolini will appreciate something of the highly charged emotions likely to have been on display at this harrowing event.

A journey to a crucifixion was a wretched one for the prisoners, the ugly nature of the scene and those participating in the spectacle being evoked with incredible intensity in the painting *Christ Carrying the Cross,* the precise artist for this work being unknown but believed to be by a follower of Hieronymous Bosch (dating from between 1500–1535). The condemned men had been forced to carry heavy rough-hewn wooden crosses through the city[37] and had now arrived at the place of their execution in the knowledge that what awaited them was to be a long drawn-out and excruciatingly painful death. There were the soldiers with paraphernalia to do the deed, as well as the usual swords and spears, for they had to be ever-ready lest a rescue attempt be made, they had whips, iron nails, hammers, axes, pincers, ladders, a crow-bar and iron mallet, as well as rope to help them hoist up the

---

36 Pasolini is believed to have chosen Matthew's Gospel as Jesus comes across as a more militant and political figure. The following academic paper is well worth reading in this regard: Mugnai, M. (2014). Pier Paolo Pasolini's "Mandatory Challenge": Jesus from "La ricotta" to "The Gospel According to Saint Matthew". *Italica, 91*(3), pp. 437–449.

37 Jesus's route to crucifixion is often commemorated in a series of images collectively known as the Stations of the Cross. His journey to execution is frequently described as taking place along the Via Dolorosa (Latin for 'Way of Grief' or 'Way of Sorrows').

crosses. Some artistic works spare the viewer little of the horror of the scene, with emphasis placed on the grimaces of those having their hands and feet transpierced with nails. Others seek to emphasise the crowd and focus on the primary reason that they were at Golgotha that day. Jörg Breu the Elder's *The Raising of the Cross* (1524) manages to capture the dramatic moment when Jesus is being hoisted up next to Dismas. Not all depictions feature the Latin Cross, a rather powerful painting of the Crucifixion of Christ known as the *Wiltern Crucifixion* (1453) by an unknown Tyrolean artist features T-shaped crosses, as well as including many of those depicted in the attire of the fifteenth century.

Historically artists and writers have portrayed a bleak, forbidding and rocky landscape, one that is desolate and devoid of hope. Artists in different parts of the world have drawn inspiration from local landscapes and climatic conditions to convey the scene, with Russell Drysdale's *Crucifixion* (1946) being heavily influenced by his experience of an extreme drought in New South Wales, Australia in 1944. Invariably the weather is used by artists to fit the mood, with doleful or angry skies darkening as the day progresses. This use of pathetic fallacy reminds the faithful that before the light of the Resurrection and Ascension must first come the utter blackness of the Crucifixion. Karel van Mander the Elder's *Landscape with snow and the Crucifixion* (1599), whilst using some poetic license in featuring snow skilfully manages to capture the stark and hostile nature of the locale.

The public execution of criminals was a common sight across the Roman Empire, but this one was different in view of the way that Jesus was perceived and treated. Pontius Pilate instructed that a *titulus* was nailed above Jesus's head, it read: INRI – the Latin inscription IESVS NAZARENVS REX IVDÆORVM (Iesus Nazarenus, Rex Iudaeorum), which in English translates as "Jesus the Nazarene, King of the Jews"

6 *Crucifixion* (1946) – Russell Drysdale, Art Gallery NSW, Sydney, Australia.
The artist has drawn heavily on his experience of a severe drought in Australia to
convey the bleak and hostile nature of the landscape, which also seems appropriate
as those crucified would have suffered terribly from dehydration. This post-war work
has a post-apocalyptic feel to it.

(Matthew 27:37; Mark 15:26; Luke 23:38 and John 19:19). John's Gospel
tells us that this superscription was written in Hebrew, Latin, and
Greek (John 19:20). The film *The Passion of the Christ* (2004) endeavours
to capture the multilingual aspect of the Crucifixion and the events
that proceeded it by using Hebrew, Latin, and reconstructed Aramaic.
Crucifixion (1880) by Thomas Eakins is a *tour de force* of Realism, that
not only reveals a thorough understanding of human physiology, it
also manages to remain true to what is known of a crucifixion, such
as the fact that four nails were used, rather than the three featured
in many works of art. Many artists have opted for portraying Christ's
crucifixion singly, or in the case of a work of 1912 by Jindřich Průcha
with Jesus's cross given greater prominence, and the thieves set
back, with one cross, presumably that of the Impenitent Thief as it

7   *Landscape with snow and the Crucifixion* (1599) – Karel van Mander, Private Collection. This panoramic Crucifixion is believed to have been based on an earlier work of 1517 by Lucas van Leyden and uses a Flemish winter snowscape to heighten the contrast between dark and light.

is on Christ's left, largely obscured. Down the ages there have been both stylised and realistic interpretations of the Crucifixion, some featuring the Crown of Thorns and a bloodied and bruised figure of Christ, others are pared down and minimalist in nature, sombre yet reverential, homing in on Jesus in his time of trial and tribulation.

The interplay of those present at the Crucifixion has been recorded in diverse ways. The contrast between Christ and those there to savour his humiliation has not been lost on artists, that said, it is difficult for most artists to capture the moment when Jesus said; *"Father, forgive them; for they know not what they do."* (Luke 23:34). In the visions of the Blessed Anne Catherine Emmerich (1774–1824) recorded in *The Dolorous Passion of Our Lord Jesus Christ*[38]; *"Dismas (the good thief) was silent but he was deeply moved at the prayer of Jesus for his enemies."* [39]

---

[38] This work of piety has been the subject of some discussion around its provenance and authenticity.
[39] Emmerich, A. *The Dolorous Passion of Our Lord Jesus Christ*, Chapter XLII – Available at: www.ecatholic2000.com/anne/passion57.shtml [Accessed 24 March 2020]

Maybe this was the point of revelation for the Good Thief. The Gospels refer to the fact that when the crosses were erected Jesus was placed in the centre and thus being both the centre point and Christ-centred. Jesus is often painted with a nimbus around his head and light used to represent the Deity of Christ.

Since the Middle Ages artistic works portraying the Passion of Christ have usually placed Dismas (The Good Thief) on the *dexter* (right) side of Jesus and Gestas (The Bad Thief) on the *sinister* side, that is to the left. The exquisite Book of Hours – *The Trés Riches Heures du Duc de Berry* (circa 1410) and the magnificent Renaissance fresco of *The Crucifixion* by Gaudenzio Ferrari (completed 1513) in *La Chiesa di Santa Maria delle Grazie* (The Church of Our Lady of the Graces), Varalla Sesia, Piedmont, Italy are typical of those works that depict this arrangement.

Frequently in artistic portrayals of the Crucifixion Christ's head is inclined towards the right. To be on a person's right-hand side has long been deemed to be a place of honour. Artistic portrayals of the Crucifixion such as that in the Church of Debra Berhan Selassie, Gondar, Ethiopia routinely place the Good Thief, as well as the Virgin Mary to the right of the crucified Christ.

Dismas often has his head raised and his eyes looking towards the face of the Saviour, as the central cross is invariably placed on raised ground. Titian's arresting *Christ and the Good Thief* (circa 1561) portrays an animated Dismas seemingly having experienced self-realisation and conversion as he looks across at the luminous, yet exhausted figure of Christ. In some works of art there is a skull placed at the base of the Cross of Christ; this is symbolic of the fact that it was believed that Adam had been buried in the vicinity of Golgotha and also serves as a reminder of Adam and Eve, the Garden of Eden, and of

Original Sin[40]; with the crucifixion of Jesus (the new Adam) enabling mankind to start afresh and be reconciled with God. *The Crucifixion* by Andrea Mantegna, completed circa 1459, features a skull at the foot of the Cross, as well as including visual clues that make clear that the place of execution was within easy reach of Jerusalem.

There is often use of evocative lighting, with some artists choosing to portray Dismas as quite a handsome figure with a halo or with angels hovering above as if ready to escort his soul in the form of a baby to heaven, an example being Giotto di Bondone's scene of the *Crucifixion* (circa 1330) that is now exhibited in the Louvre Museum, Paris. Historically Gestas is often pictured with exaggerated Semitic features, with Satan or a winged demonic fiend above him snatching his soul to deliver it to perdition. Jacopo di Cione's altaipiece with the *Crucifixion* (1369–70) in the National Gallery, London features on Christ's right a behaloed Dismas and on his left Gestas being tormented by two devilish fiends holding a brazier above his head – emblematic of the fires of hell. Rembrandt van Rijn's *Christ Crucified between the Two Thieves: The Three Crosses* (1653) is a veritable triumph that uses a combination of etching and dry point to portray Divine Light illuminating the figure of Christ. One of the most moving portayals of Dismas on the cross is a fresco of the *Crucifixion* (completed in 1442) by Giovanni da Fiesole, known as Fra Angelico, and is in the Chapter House of the Dominican Covent of San Marco, Florence, Italy. A youthful looking Penitent Thief has a serene, beatific calm about him as he looks across at Jesus Christ, for this scene captures the moment that the thief hears the Messiah's promise: *"Truly, I say to you, today you will be with me in Paradise."* (Luke 23:43). In the Holy Door (1950) of St.

---

40 Original Sin has long been a contentious issue amongst theologians and remains a moot point between different Christian churches.

8 *Crucifixion* (1880) – Thomas Eakins, Philadelphia Museum of Art, Philadelphia, USA. This Nineteenth century masterpiece of Realism features a number of details of Christ's crucifixion that are believed to have been accurate, these include a *suppedaneum* (foot-support) and the fact that four nails were used, rather than three as often portrayed in many works of art.

9   Crucifixion (1912) – Jindřich Průcha, National Gallery, Prague, Czech Republic. There is evidence of Expressionism in this sombre work. Průcha was killed at the Battle of Komarów during the early months of the First World War.

Peter's Basilica, Rome one of a series of bronze panels designed by the sculptor Vico Consorti features Christ looking across and speaking to Dismas and includes the Latin inscription: *Hodie Mecum Eris In Paradiso* (Today you will be with me in Paradise). Another magnificent fresco that encapsulates the drama and symbolism of the *Crucifixion* dates from 1529 and is by Bernardino Luini and is to be found in the Church of Santa Maria degli Angeli, Lugano, Switzerland.

There is some discussion as to whether those executed were naked; there is every likelihood that they were as this would further demean and humiliate them. The two thieves were almost certainly naked, yet it is possible to surmise from the tenor of Pontius Pilate's conversations with Jesus that he might have wished Jesus to keep at least some semblance of dignity. That said, historic religious sensitivities around

10 *The Crucifixion* (15ᵗʰ century) Les Très Riches Heures du duc de Berry, Folio 152v, The Condé Museum, Chantilly, France. Books of Hours of this nature and quality contained images that were intended to be a means of devotion and prayer. Here Dismas can clearly be seen looking earnestly at Christ.

11 *Crucifixion fresco* (1513) – Gaudenzio Ferrari, The Church of Our Lady of the Graces, Varalla Sesia, Piedmont, Italy. The fate of the two thieves is made clear by what accompanies them, be it angels to transport the soul to Heaven or a foul fiend intent on torment.

nudity and its portrayal have resulted in the majority of works of art that have portayed the Crucifixion showing Jesus and the thieves wearing loincloths to avoid causing offence. During the Victorian period prudery compounded such an approach, with the added dimension that Jesus Christ was often depicted, almost certainly erroneously, as having been blue-eyed and with blonde or flaxen hair. Decidedly Caucasian-looking depictions of Jesus, where his ethnicity is effectively photoshopped distorts the reality, something that often results in preconceptions and misconceptions about him, his life, death, and Resurrection. *The Wales Window for Alabama* by John Petts (1964) is a striking example of how a medium such as stained glass can embody different meanings and identities. In recent years, some artists have quite deliberately used models of contrasting ethnicities to portray Jesus as a reminder to the world that he is not the preserve of any one race or culture.

Crucifixion was designed to be a slow and painful death. Successive generations of artists have endeavoured to capture the pain and agony of those executed, with Jesus being their primary focus. *Crucifixion* (1946)[41] by Graham Sutherland is a powerful yet grim work that resulted in part from the fact that the artist drew deeply on the visual imagery of and his visceral reaction to the photographs and newsreel footage that emerged following the liberation of Concentration Camps such as Bergen-Belsen at the end of the Second World War. A reminder of the horrors and blasphemies that mankind has perpetrated throughout history.

The Gospels not only tell of the passage of time, thus intimating the unimaginable suffering, but also how the sky darkened during the Crucifixion. Light and darkness plays a symbolic role, primarily

---

41 A fine version of this work is to be found in St. Matthew's Church, Northampton, UK –
www.stmatthewsnorthampton.org.uk/art_history_the_crucifixion.shtml

12 *The Crucifixion*, Church of Debra Berhan Selassie, Gondar, Ethiopia. The name of the church means The Light of the Trinity in Amharic. Close observance of this Crucifixion scene reveals a darkened or eclipsed sun and a reddened moon, both celestial signs of portentous events.

13 *Christ and the Good Thief* (circa 1561) – Titian, The National Art Gallery of Bologna, Italy. This work is believed to be by Tiziano Vecellio, better known as Titian. The skilful use of light in the Good Thief's visible right eye connotes so much more than sight.

14 *Crucifixion* (circa 1459) – Andrea Mantegna, The Louvre Museum, Paris, France. Mantegna's eye for detail is quite extraordinary; the care taken over the Roman soldiers for instance speaks volumes.

15 *Crucifixion* (circa 1330) - Giotto di Bondone, The Louvre Museum, Paris, France. Giotto leaves the viewer in no doubt who the Good Thief is, the thief to the right of Christ has a halo. Take note of the careful way in which a trio of figures are in the process of gambling over Jesus's garments.

16 *The Crucifixion* (1369/70) – Jacopo di Cione, The National Gallery, London, UK. The wounds of Christ are often a cause for reflection and reverence and this masterpiece of Florentine art ensures that they are indeed an area of focus. That said, it is interesting to note that none of those crucified show any signs of having been scourged.

17 *Christ Crucified between Two Thieves: The Three Crosses* (1653) – Rembrandt van Rijn, Metropolitan Museum of Arts, New York, USA. Rembrandt reworked this masterpiece through various print runs. It is worth noting that unusually the Good Thief and the Virgin Mary are both portrayed on the viewers right.

with the darkening sky as a portent of Jesus's imminent death and a reminder of the wider significance of the events that were unfolding. Accompanying the horror of the Crucifixion are scenes such as the soldiers casting lots[42] for the clothes of Jesus (Matthew 27:35; Mark 15:24; Luke 23:34 and John 19:24), or the scene of someone hurrying to find a sponge and vinegar to offer it up on a stick to a dehydrated and dying Jesus (Matthew 27:48; Mark 15:36 and John 19:30). There is the high drama of Jesus crying out to His father (Matthew 27:46; Mark

---

42 Artists invariably depict this as the soldiers playing dice, an example being the mural painted in 1959/60 by Jean Cocteau in the Lady Chapel of Notre Dame de France, Soho, London.

15: 34 and Luke 23:46), and his exclaiming; *"It is finished"* (John 19:30), a moment conveyed in a woodcut print by Augustin Kolb (1869–1942) entitled *Crucifixion: My work is done.* Jesus having been crucified at 9 o'clock (the third hour) in the morning, the sky began to darken at 12 noon (the sixth hour) and his death at 3 o'clock (the ninth hour). The moment of Jesus Christ's death being marked by dramatic events described in Matthew's Gospel:

"And behold, the curtain of the temple was torn in two, from top to bottom; and the earth shook, and the rocks were split; the tombs also were opened, and many bodies of the saints who had fallen asleep were raised, and coming out of the tombs after his resurrection they went into the holy city and appeared to many. When the centurion and those who were with him, keeping watch over Jesus, saw the earthquake and what took place, they were filled with awe, and said, 'Truly this was the Son of God!' " (Matthew 27:51–54).

Students of dramaturgy would find the placing, interplay, and representation of the various characters fascinating. This momentous historic event continues to inspire dramatic portrayals of the Crucifixion such as the *Passionsspiele Oberammergau* (The Oberammergau Passion Play) that has been perfomed in Bavaria, Germany since 1634.

Many artistic representations of Jesus's death focus on the darkness of the deed and of the setting. Matthew's Gospel recounts that at the very moment the Son of Man died darkness swept over the land for three hours (Matthew 27:45). Some artworks have almost taken on a quasi-eschatological dimension, whilst darkness and light are a perennial theme in artistic representatives of the Crucifixion. Dirck Volkertsz Coornhert's etching *The Crucifixion of Christ* (1548) uses light and shade to marvellous effect to capture the trauma and upheaval of the occasion. The sun and moon sometimes feature in works of art whether these be of the Eastern or Western tradition; these have an allegorical purpose and provide a cosmic dimension to the narrative. The coloration featured appears to echo the following passage from The Revelation to John which is understood to refer to the events at Christ's crucifixion:

"When he opened the sixth seal, I looked and behold, there was a great earthquake; and the sun became black as sackcloth, the full moon became like blood and the stars of the sky fell to earth as the fig tree sheds its winter fruit when shaken by a gale;" (Revelation 6:12–13)

It is believed that following Jesus's death both thieves were found to be still alive nearly three hours later. As it was Paraseve (Mark 15:42) the Jews prevailed upon Pontius Pilate to ensure that those still living were finished off and their bodies taken down before the commencement of the Sabbath (John 19:31). Soldiers were duly ordered before sunset to carry out *crurifragium* (the breaking of legs) of the criminals to hasten their death (John 19:32). John's Gospel recounts how soldiers checked that Jesus was dead by piercing his side with a spear (John 19:34).[43] The Master of the Rajhrad Altarpiece (1420), now in the National Gallery in Prague, features a soldier about to break Dismas's legs, whilst an angel is on hand to carry his soul heavenward. A Seventeenth century icon of the Cretan School in the State Hermitage Museum, St. Petersburg, Russia, also features Gestas having his legs broken; the Crucifixion scene features a host of other important elements including Mary Magdalene in red weeping at the foot of Jesus's cross and an angel holding a chalice to catch the blood from the lance/spear wound on his right side.

---

43 Jesus Christ's legs were not broken, and this is seen as a fulfilment of the Scriptures (John 19:36–37).

In the Gospels there is no further mention of the Penitent and the Impenitent Thieves or what happened to their mortal remains. Jesus's body was at least spared further indignity when Joseph of Arimathea asked for and was granted permission by the Roman Governor to collect the corpse and take it away for a decent burial (Matthew 27:57–60; Mark 15:42–46; Luke 23:50–55 and John 19:38–42).[44] The taking down of Jesus from the Cross, known as the *Descent from the Cross* or the *Deposition of Christ*, is sensitively captured in the Hofer Alterpiece (1465) by Hans Pleydenwurff. In the *Cinquecento* a popular, if sometimes controversial, motif associated with artistic depictions of the *Descent from the Cross* was *Lo Spasimo* – the swoon of the Virgin Mary.[45] One of the most moving subjects in Christian art (especially sculpture) is a *pietà* (Italian for "pity" or "compassion") portraying the Virgin Mary cradling the dead body of Jesus. *La Piedad* (Spanish for *"pity"*) by the Spanish Baroque sculptor Gregorio Fernández (1616) in the *Museo Nacional De Escultura* (National Museum of Sculpture), Valladolid, Spain is typical of this genre.

The iconography of the Crucifixion has been adapted and changed over time and continues to reflect certain artistic schools, vernacular traditions, and religious and cultural sensitivities. Holy sites and relics have been revered and the focus of pilgrimage and artistic adornment[46].

---

44 *The Site That May Be Jesus' Tomb* provides some sense of the distances involves – Available at: www.nationalgeographic.com/magazine/2017/12/was-this-jesus-tomb/ [Accessed 18 April 2020]

45 Hamburgh, H. (1981). The Problem of Lo Spasimo of the Virgin in Cinquecento Paintings of the Descent from the Cross. *The Sixteenth Century Journal, 12*(4), pp. 45–75.

46 The Basilica di Santa Croce in Gerusalemme (The Basilica of the Holy Cross in Jersalem) in Rome contains fragments purported to be from the True Cross as well as a piece of the Penitent Thief's cross labelled *Pars Crucis Boni Latronis* (Part of the Cross of the Good Thief).

The Crucifixion is reflected in a range of art forms such as the Roman Catacombs, Orthodox iconastasis, medieval psalters, Victorian stained glass and cinematic and modern art. Artists endeavour to capture a bittersweet scene, that to many is painfully beautiful; a powerful synthesis of degradation and beauty, shame and glory, and suffering and hope.

DISMAS AND THE VIRGIN MARY

In the Catholic Church St. Dismas is commemorated on 25th March, the same day as the Feast of the Annunciation of the Blessed Virgin Mary, when Christ was conceived and so became Incarnate. Historically, therefore, Good Friday took place on the same day as the Annunciation, and, in the ancient mind, on the same day as Creation itself. Spiritual coincidence and serendipity of this nature stimulates considerable thought and deliberation, especially as there are obvious mystical connections.

Christ's Sacrifice on the Cross presages and embodies a new creation, one that enables the salvation of mankind. The association with the Annunciation is a powerful reminder that Jesus Christ is starting creation anew, in a dynamic and constructive way. Through Christ mankind and indeed the world is restored from within, and individuals such as Dismas are saved. Some Biblical scholars and theologians recognise echoes of the meaning and symbolism of Adam and the Garden of Eden: knowledge, promises and fulfilment all play their part. The Catholic belief that Mary the Mother of Jesus is his Gate of Heaven and that she is the Refuge of Sinners has resulted in added synergy between Mary and Dismas.

An encounter between Mary and some criminals during the Holy Family's Flight into Egypt is first mentioned in the *Syriac Infancy*

18 *Crucifixion fresco* (1442) – Fra Angelico, Convent of San Marco, Florence, Italy. A deeply contemplative piece in which a youthful Dismas looks across at Christ in an almost beatific manner. Note that none of the crucified figures appear to have been scourged.

19 *Holy Door* (1950) – Vico Consorti, St Peter's Basilica, Rome, Italy. This panel featuring the Good Thief receiving the assurance from Jesus is one of sixteen cast by the Ferdinando Marinelli Artistic Foundry, Florence.

20 *Crucifixion fresco* (1529) –
Bernardino Luini, Church
of Santa Maria degli Angeli, Lugano,
Switzerland. A mastery work that
is alive with detail. Note the soldiers
in dispute over Jesus's scarlet robe and
the angel above Dismas holding a baby
– emblematic of his soul.

**21 *The Wales Window
for Alabama*** (1964) – John Pett,
16th Street Baptist Church, Birmingham,
Alabama, USA. Photograph by Jeffrey
Isaac Greenberg. To have a stained
glass window which depicted Christ
as black was a radical departure from
most of the visual representations
of Jesus. This striking creation has
a tragic back story yet is a symbol
of solidarity and hope.

22 *Crucifixion* –
Graham Sutherland
(1946). Vatican
Museum, Rome, Italy.
A preparatory study
for a harrowing work
that drew heavily upon
the disturbing footage
that emerged from
the recently liberated
Nazi concentration
camps. Sutherland took
inspiration from the
Isenheim Altarpiece
(circa 1515) by
Matthias Grunewald.

23 *Soldiers playing dice in the Crucifixion mural* (1959/60) by Jean Cocteau,
Notre Dame de France, Soho, London, UK. – Photograph by Mark Thomas Jones.
Cocteau included himself in this Crucifixion mural, he is to the right of the shield
bearing the eagle.

24 *The Crucifixion of Christ* (1548) – Dirck Volkertsz Coornhert, Rijksmuseum, Amsterdam, The Netherlands. Whilst Coornhert has exaggerated the muscles and sinews somewhat, the energy and dynamism in this piece is palpable. Note the way in which the sun and moon are featured.

25 *Crucifixion: My work is done* – Augustin Kolb (1869-1942), Cleveland Museum of Art, Cleveland, USA. The physicality of this woodcut is quite remarkable. The Crown of Thorns skilfully feeds into the light burst vector of Christ's halo.

26 *Crucifixion* (1420) – Master of the Rajhrad Altarpiece, National Gallery, Prague, Czech Republic. At the commencement of the Hussite Wars an anonymous painter worked on a larger winged altar originally destined for the Church of St. Maurice, Olomouc. Of the six surviving paintings, five later found their way to the Benedictine monastery at Rajhrad, hence the name.

27 Crucifixion – Cretan School Icon featuring Adam's skull (17th century), State Hermitage Museum, St. Petersburg, Russia. Directly to the right of Adam's skull at the foot of Christ's cross can be seen the centurion Longinus with a lance; this Roman soldier famously exclaimed; *"Truly, this man was the son of God!"* (Mark 15:38). In some Christian churches Longinus is regarded as a saint.

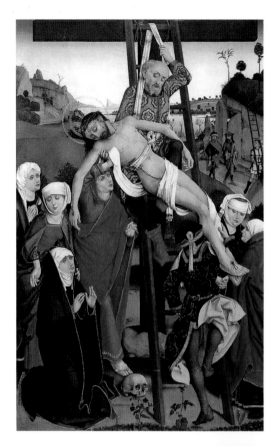

28 Hofer altarpiece
(1465) – Hans Pleydenwurff,
Alte Pinakothek, Munich,
Germany. The sensitivity and
reverence of this piece is quite
something. The composition
and detail on the fabrics
featured is redolent of some of
the finest work of the Northern
Renaissance.

29 La Piedad (1616) – Gregorio
Fernández, National Museum
of Sculpture, Valladolid, Spain.
This work formed part of a *paso*
(an elaborate religious float) that
was carried reverently through
the streets during Holy Week.
It was commissioned by a Catholic
fraternity, the Illustrious Brotherhood
of Our Lady of Anguish.

Gospels[47] and the *Gospel of Nicodemus* and later expanded upon by St. Anselm. In this latter narrative Dismas the criminal demonstrates another side to his character when he recognises the sanctity of Jesus and gives charity to Him and Mary and Joseph. A key aspect of the story is that the Virgin Mary assures Dismas that he will be rewarded for his kindness shortly before his death. For all his apparent sinfulness there is the whole theological debate about the role of good works in being a route to Salvation; this brings to mind the line from Scripture: *"You see then that a man is justified by works and not by faith only."* (James 2:24). In Catholic hagiology Jesus's mother has a pivotal role to play, as Dismas for all his nefarious activity before and after first encountering the Holy Family receives the Motherly Mercy of Mary at the Crucifixion. Imagine, if you will, the impact that the Good Thief's defence of Jesus's innocence might have had upon Mary. Mary the Mediatrix recognises Dismas and intercedes for him. Here we would do well to appreciate that Divine forgiveness is a gift, not a reward. Mary's sublime function as a mediator between God and humanity is a frequent area of study in Mariology. Catholics believe that the Grace of Mary was instrumental in Dismas's salvation and this is reflected in the status Dismas is given by the Catholic Church, as well as in artistic representations of the Crucifixion.

In Catholicism it has been a pious tradition to call the Penitent Thief, Dismas and as St. Dismas he is often portrayed as being muscular, sometimes bearded, wearing a loincloth, either holding his cross or being crucified, or on occasions standing in Paradise. There

---

47 Cornelia Horn's exploration and analysis of Ancient Syriac sources sheds considerable light onto the understanding of the Virgin Mary's perceived role as an intercessor. Horn, C. (2015). Ancient Syriac Sources on Mary's Role as Intercessor. In Peltomaa L., Külzer A., & Allen P. (Eds.), *Presbeia Theothokou: The Intercessory Role of Mary across Times and Places in Byzantium (4th–9th Century)* (pp. 153–176). Vienna: Austrian Academy of Sciences Press.

is no uniform way of portaying the Good Thief, some artists have chosen to depict him as a relatively slim, physically unblemished, and youthful looking figure. He has long had a relatively small, but loyal following in the Catholic Church, with evidence of marked devotion in Central Europe since the Seventeenth Century in places such as Bohemia, Lower Austria and Styria,[48] believed to have been fostered by the Franciscans and the Jesuits. The deaths of the two thieves has frequently been used as an object lesson with the English Jesuit theologian William Darrell (1651 – 1721) writing in *The Gentleman Instructed in the Conduct of a Virtuous and Happy Life* (1704); *"I counsell all Christians to draw this conclusion from the different deaths of these two malefactors, that it is madness to despair, and temerity to presume,".*[49]

In respect of the Crucifixion, Mary is often portrayed standing with the other womenfolk on the left-hand side of a painting in front of Dismas who is facing outwards or who is looking towards her son. Thus, to Jesus as he looks down from the Cross, his mother is on the right in a place of honour even in the time of his degradation and death. Both Dismas and Mary are on the same side of Christ as the spear-wound from which poured forth the blood (of the Eucharist) and water (of baptism).[50] Dismas undergoes the physical agony whilst Mary suffers the emotional anguish, trauma, and sorrow of losing her son. The pathos of the drama continues to cause the devout to reflect and inspires sublime music such as the setting of the *Stabat Mater*

48 Timmermann, A. (2014). "Locus calvariae": Walking and Hanging with Christ and the Good Thief, c. 1350 – c. 1700. *Artibus Et Historiae, 35*(69), pp. 137–161.
49 Darrell, W. (1704). *The Gentleman Instructed in the Conduct of a Virtuous and Happy Life,* E. Evets, London.
50 Some scholars and scientists have endeavoured to explain the presence of water by claiming that what in fact poured forth was pericardial fluid, as the spear or lance would have pierced the pericardium, a thin sack that surrounds the heart.

by Giovanni Battista Pergolesi (1710–1736). In recent times the use of the name Dismas amongst Catholics has fallen into desuetude in the popular vocabulary, but the special association between the Good Thief and the Virgin Mary endures.

The following is a prayer of Pope Pius XII (1876–1958):

> *O Sacred Heart of Jesus,*
> *make us love Thee more and more.*
> *Our Lady of Hope, pray for us.*
> *Saint Dismas, the Good Thief, pray for us.*[51]

THE GOOD THIEF
AND DIFFERENT WORSHIP TRADITIONS

Whilst not every denomination accepts the legend of Dismas's encounter with and generosity to the Holy Family, the part played by the Penitent Thief in the Crucifixion is seen as enormously significant and has resonated widely. Orthodox, Coptic, Catholic and Protestant churches have found much in his example of a sinner who sees the light and acknowledges Jesus in the way that he does. Awareness of personal sin, repentance, and acceptance of Christ and the fact that Salvation comes through him are all lessons that are drawn from one sometimes referred to as the Good Thief. Whereas theologians may argue about whether salvation is possible without good works, a strong case can be made that the Penitent Thief does indeed do a good work in the form of his final witness and act of acknowledgment. He challenges Gestas, his co-criminal and by so doing differentiates himself. Some

---

51 A Saint for Prisoners: Dismas – Available at: http://biblesaints.blogspot.com/2011/03/saint-for-prisoners-dismas.html [Accessed 2 April 2020]

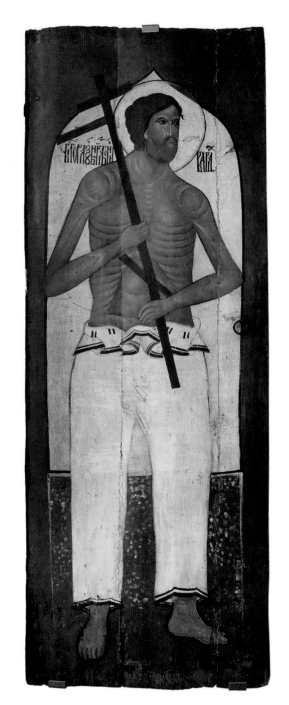

30 *Good Thief Icon*
(16th century), Rostov
Kremlin, Russia. The
icon is believed to have
originally been part of
the Tolgskaya icon of
Our Lady in Rostov.
The Good Thief is
sometimes known as
the Prudent Robber in
the Orthodox Church.

31 *The Collegiate Church of the Ikon of the Mother of God Joy of All Who Sorrow*, Mettingham, Suffolk, UK – Photograph by Simon Knott. An icon of the Good Thief (carrying his cross) is deliberately placed to serve as a reminder to all that only by our sincere admission of our sin and acknowledgement of the supremacy of Jesus Christ will Salvation be possible.

32 *St. Dismas Icon door, The Collegiate Church of the Ikon of the Mother of God Joy of All Who Sorrow*, Mettingham, Suffolk, UK – Photograph by Simon Knott. This icon is a visual reminder of God's Grace.

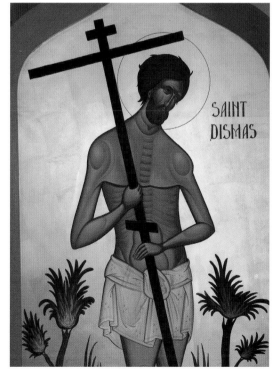

SAINT DISMAS

might say that he reveals not only an empathy for Jesus, but a supreme love, even in the depths of his own suffering. Dismas's moment of revelation, of self-realisation and acknowledgement of the Righteous One secures him a place in Paradise; a fulfilment of the promise made by Jesus Christ: "*So every one who acknowledges me before men, I also will acknowledge before my Father who is in heaven;* (Matthew 10:32). The theological debate about the role of good works or whether one can attain Salvation by faith alone remains a bone of contention. That said, the *clara visio* that the Penitent Thief demonstrates, albeit in his final hours, has helped make him an exemplar who is held up, to differing degrees, in daily worship across the world.

As Jesus during his three years of ministry had sought out those that society had shunned, condemned or seen as only worthy of contempt, it seems strangely apposite that at the end of his earthly life he should be among both Jew and Gentile, believer and unbeliever, and be placed between criminals who are dubbed penitent and impenitent. The Reverend James Rudge D.D.[52] in a sermon of 1839 entitled: *The Believer Crucified with Christ* spoke of Jesus's death on the Cross having; "*broken down the partition-wall between Jew and Gentile, and taken it away, nailing it to his cross.*"[53] It is noteworthy that it is one of the Gentiles, a Roman soldier, who recognises Christ's true nature (Matthew 27:54, Mark 15:39 and Luke 23:47) and it is Dismas who comes to Jesus's defence. In the Armenian Chapel of St. Helena, Jerusalem there is an apse containing an altar dedicated to St. Dismas. In the Armenian Church one of the most revered prayers is one entitled *I Confess With Faith*; it is twenty-

---

52 D.D. is the abbreviation for Doctor of Divinity, the holder of an advanced or honorary academic degree in divinity (the study of religion; theology).

53 Rudge, J. (1839). The Believer Crucified with Christ, *The Church of England Magazine*, Jan-June, pp.186–193.

four verses long and was written in the Twelfth century by Nerses Shnorlali, known as Nerses IV the Gracious (1102–1173); the fourth verse mentions Christ's promise made to the Good Thief:

> *"Son of God, true God,*
> *Who descended from the bosom of the Father,*
> *And took on flesh from the holy virgin Mary for our salvation,*
> *Who was crucified, buried and rose from the dead,*
> *And ascended with glory to the Father.*
> *I have sinned against heaven and before you.*
> *Remember me as you did the penitent thief*
> *when you come with your kingdom.*
> *Have mercy upon your creation,*
> *And on me, a manifold sinner."*[54]

The Penitent Thief also receives some attention in the Ethiopian[55] and Eritrean Orthodox Tewahedo Church, and mention in the Paschal matins of Eastern Orthodox Tradition where much is made of the Catechetical Homily of St. John Chrysostom about the fact that it is never too late to turn to Christ. Moreover, acknowledgement is made of both voluntary and involuntary transgressions and significantly the supplication of the Wise Thief, as he is usually known to the Orthodox, is remembered in the following prayer that is always used in the Orthodox Church prior to Communion:

---

54 I Confess with Faith – St. Nerses Shnorhali the Gracious – Available at: https://shnorhali.com/english/ [Accessed 4 April 2020]

55 The Ethiopian Orthodox Church uses the New Testament Apocrypha of the Syriac Infancy Gospel; therefore, the Good and Bad thieves are called Titus (ጢጦስ/Ti'tos) and Dumachus (ዱማስ/Dukas) respectively. I have included the Amharic name to communicate the fact that the names have a slightly different intonation when pronounced in Amharic.

"Receive me today, Son of God, as a partaker of Your mystical Supper. I will not reveal Your mystery to Your adversaries. Nor will I give You a kiss as did Judas. But as the thief I confess to You: Lord, remember me in Your kingdom."[56]

The Good Thief's words are remembered in the *Kathisma Hymn (Tone 8)* that may be sung as part of the preparation for the Holy Communion:

"May my receiving of Thine immaculate and life-creating Mysteries, O Savior, be as fire and light for me, burning up the chaff of my sins and enlightening me to proclaim the true God; for I will not give Thy holy things to the deceiving enemy neither will I kiss Thee in deceit, but like the sinful woman will I fall down before Thee and confess Thee as the thief; crying out: "Remember me, O Lord, in Thy kingdom!"[57][58]

Similarly, at the Taizé Community, an ecumenical Christian monastic fraternity in Taizé, Saône-et-Loire, Burgundy, France a frequent prayer is: *"Jesus, remember me, when you come into your kingdom."*[59]

56 Before and after Holy Communion – Orthodox Church in America – Available at: www.oca.org/orthodoxy/prayers/before-and-after-holy-communion [Accessed 18 March 2020]
57 Before Communion Prayers – St John Orthodox Church – Available at: www.ocanwa.org/prayers-before-holy-communion [Accessed 18 March 2020]
58 With reference to the wording of prayers used prior to Holy Communion, one challenge is that there is no common translation across the Orthodox jurisdictions in the English-speaking world. Diaspora communities in the Anglosphere and elsewhere face a range of challenges that are sometimes mirrored in the way the Orthodox Church functions locally. The following paper elucidates some of the issues: Thorbjørnsrud, B. (2015). "The Problem of the Orthodox Diaspora": The Orthodox Church between Nationalism, Transnationalism, and Universality. *Numen, 62*(5/6), pp.568–595. Other churches also wrestle with the types of issues raised in this article.
59 Taizé – Available at: www.taize.fr/en [Accessed 20 March 2020]

Direct liturgical reference to the Wise Thief occurs in the Orthodox Matins of Great and Holy Friday, which is served by 'anticipation' on the Thursday evening. This service is often referred to as *The Twelve Gospels* since twelve gospel passages are read during its course and normally, this service lasts about three and a half hours.

The 14th Antiphon (these antiphons are a series of hymns between the first six Gospel readings) focuses on the Wise Thief:

> *"The thief, whose hands, were defiled with blood,*
> *Thou didst accept as Thy fellow traveller.*
> *With him number us also, O Lord,*
> *For Thou art good and lovest mankind.*

> *The thief on the Cross uttered a small cry,*
> *But he found great faith.*
> *In a moment he was saved*
> *And became the first to enter Paradise*
> *When its gates were opened.*
> *O Lord who didst accept his repentance, glory to Thee!"*

Similarly, during the Beatitudes which are read with 'inter-verses' after the sixth Gospel references to the Wise Thief appear, making sharp contrasts with other characters in the narrative and eventually identification with those engaged in worship. Echoing the request in Luke 23:42 with the words; *"Remember us also, O Saviour in thy Kingdom!"* Thus, as the reading of the Beatitudes progresses the words of the Wise Thief; *"Jesus, remember me when you come into your kingly power."* are taken into the heart of the people, since the text suggests that we identify ourselves as the Wise Thief.

"When it beheld Thee crucified, O Christ, all creation trembled. The foundations of the earth shook for fear of Thy Might. The lights of heaven hid themselves and the curtain of the temple was torn in two. The mountains quaked, and the rocks were split, and with us the believing thief cried out to Thee, O Saviour: Remember me in Thy Kingdom!"

Immediately before the Ninth Gospel reading the *Exaposteilarion* (The Hymn of Light) is sung three times:

"The wise thief didst Thou make worthy of Paradise
in a single moment, O Lord;
By the wood of Thy Cross illumine me as well, and save me."[60]

This is often sung to an elaborate musical setting and is invariably the musical highlight of the service, as in many ways is the *Exaposteilarion* itself of central importance in each celebration of Matins. The Wise Thief is crucial to the Orthodox understanding, even if subconsciously for some, of salvation. An essential aspect of Orthodoxy is that of 'what we pray is what we believe' something that is meant to inform the daily lives of members of the church.

Even in the cross used by the Russian Orthodox Church the Wise Thief's fate (It is not uncommon for him to be referred to as the Prudent Robber) is commemorated. The Slavic Cross (Sometimes called the

---

60 Our Journey through Holy Week, Orthodox Church in America – Available at: www.oca.org/reflections/misc-authors/our-journey-through-holy-week [Accessed 17 March 2020]

Russian or Orthodox Cross) features a diagonal bar that symbolises firstly the wooden board to which Jesus's feet were nailed and secondly the contrasting destinies of the two thieves, with the right-hand side slanting Heavenwards and the left-hand side sloping downwards towards Hell. The revered Eastern Orthodox ascetic St. John (Maximovitch) of Shanghai and San Francisco (1896-1966) in *Why The Good Thief Was Pardoned* (1954) writes of how he was transformed at the Crucifixion; *"Gazing upon the One hanging on the Cross, he saw as in a mirror his moral downfall. All the good concealed within him was awakened and surfaced."*[61] This transformation in the state and status of the Wise Thief is something that lends itself to art used in worship. Icons[62] and iconography play an important part in Orthodox worship and has a range of purposes. An icon (from the Greek εἰκών eikōn "image", "resemblance") is a religious work of art that serves as a sacred image that may be used in religious devotion. A fine example of an icon of the Wise or Prudent Robber is part of the Tolgskaya Icon of Our Lady that is now in the Rostov Kremlin, Russia. Some Russian Orthodox churches such as the Collegiate Church of the Ikon of the Mother of God Joy of All Who Sorrow, Mettingham, Suffolk, UK feature the Good Thief as a full standing figure with a paradisiacal scene behind on one of the Deacon's Doors (the two doors at the

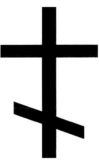

The Slavic Cross

---

61   Selected Sermons of Saint John of Shanghai and San Francisco – Available at: www. holytrinitymission.org/books/english/sermons_john_maximovich.htm [Accessed 15 March 2020]

62   In the Orthodox Christian tradition, icons are said to be written, rather than painted. The Orthodox consider making icons as more a form of prayer than art, and they believe the iconographer's hand is guided by God.

north and south end of the iconostasis leading into the sanctuary, which represents heaven).

Frequently in depictions of the Risen Lord opening the gates of paradise, there is the Penitent Thief (often known as the Wise Thief) carrying his cross, at the front of the queue, ahead of Abraham and the other Old Testament Patriachs. The irony of the scene is not lost on various believers and observers, with Aidan Hart, painter, mosaicist and carver of Sacred Icons commenting; *"I have always liked the divine humour in the thief beating all the spiritual heavies into paradise, they waiting outside while he strides in ahead."* Some have mused, albeit in jest, whether by his 'repentance' on the cross the Good Thief managed to steal paradise. A splendid example of such a sacred assemblage featuring the Wise Thief is to be found on the exterior walls of *Biserica Sfantul Gheorghe* (Church of St. George) within Voroneţ Monastery (Est. 1488), Romania.

In the Greek Orthodox Church, in *The Menaion*[63] there is no office dedicated to the Good Thief, although he is remembered with a special entry in *The Synaxarion* (The Lives of the Saints of the Orthodox Church) for the 12th October. As well as briefly describing the events of the Crucifixion it homes in on the the Good Thief remonstrating with his co-criminal, admitting his own guilt, and making his request to Jesus to be remembered. In receiving the positive response from the Messiah, it goes on to state:

"And so the Thief was the first man to obtain salvation and redemption through the Passion of Christ. He did not need years of ascesis, tears and

---

63 The Menaion is the liturgical book used by the Eastern Orthodox Church containing the propers for fixed dates of the calendar year. It is the largest volume of the propers for the Byzantine Rite and is used at nearly all the daily services.

33 Voroneţ Monastery mural, Gura Humorului, Suceava County, Romania. Sometimes known as 'the Sistine Chapel of the East', Voroneţ Monastery's murals have a vibrancy that has lasted five centuries. Internal and external imagery played an important part in the religious instruction of people in the past, as many of them were illiterate. The Good Thief (bottom left-hand corner) is depicted carrying his cross and approaching the Gates of Heaven.

prayer; his one movement of sincere repentance and his confession of Christ's divinity at the moment of the Lord's extreme humiliation, were enough to gain him possession of the good things of everlasting life."[64]

The Penitent Thief receives special reverence in the daily worship of the Coptic Orthodox Church, this is in part due to the fact that in the Fourth century AD Patriach Theophilus, the 23rd Pope of Alexandria, prepared a homily entitled: *On the Crucifixion and the Good Thief* – that constructed a dialogue between Jesus Christ and the Penitent Thief: the following is an excerpt from it:

64 Makarios, H., Petra, S. (1998) *The Synaxarion*, Vol 1, Holy Convent of The Annunciation of Our Lady Ormylia (Chalkidike), Greece, pp. 373–374.

"You have glorified me in the presence of carnal men, in the presence of sinners. I will therefore glory you in the presence of the angels. You were fixed on the cross, and you united yourself with me of your own free will."[65]

Christians in the Horn of Africa, whether they be Ethiopian or Eritrean Orthodox or Catholic hold Dismas in high regard. In Eritrea where there is approximately 90% similarity between the Orthodox and Catholic rite there is 100% agreement in the way Dismas is perceived and revered. Culturally that on the left is seen as wrong, whilst that on the right deemed "righteous". *Feyatawi Ze-yeman* ('The robber on the rightside' – of the Cross)[66] is thought of as the repentant and good robber, the very embodiment of mercy for all those who have sinned and repented. *Feyatwi Ze-Tseghan* ('The robber on the leftside' – of the Cross) is said to represent the devil for being the one who despised *Iyesus Krystios* (Jesus Christ). The use of the word "robber" rather than "thief" is significant in Eritrea as robbery is viewed as the more serious offence, therefore the more humiliating for Our Saviour to be placed between robbers[67]. In the Eritrean Catholic Holy Week liturgy there is the prayer: *Tezekerrene Ighzio Bewuste Menghsteke bekeme terekerko le Feyatawi Ze-yeman* (Lord remember us in Your Kingdom as you have forgiven the robber on the right side of your cross where you have suffered). As ever in faith and worship the lexicon and iconography matters. When compared with Protestant churches the Penitent Thief receives considerably

---

65 Scripture & Mission – Theophilus of Alexandria, Homily on the Crucifixion and the Good Thief (Excerpt 1) – Available at: https://scriptureandmission.com/2019/04/09/theophilus-of-alexandria-homily-on-the-crucifixion-and-the-good-thief-excerpt-1/ [Accessed 21 April 2020]

66 Translation kindly provided by Dr Zeremariam Fre of University College London.

67 Whilst it is important to note that Bible translations can and do vary, generally in Matthew and Mark's Gospels the two malefactors are usually described as "robbers", Luke speaks of "criminals" and John writes of Jesus being crucified "with two others". Some modern translations have chosen to use the word "rebels", which gives an added seriousness to their crimes.

more attention in the churches of the Eastern Orthodox, Oriental Orthodox[68] and Catholic tradition.

Various churches, including many of a Protestant persuasion, have seen the Salvation of the Good Thief as a fulfilment of Jesus's words as expressed in Luke's Gospel: *"...there will be more joy in heaven over one sinner who repents than over ninety-nine righteous persons who need no repentance."* (Luke 15:7) The message of grace and forgiveness resonates deeply with evangelistic churches and organisations such as The Salvation Army. Dismas's example as one who recognises Jesus's goodness and his own sin is integral to his Redemption. A problematic area has been that of good works: his case is viewed as one of *in extremis*, and so there would be an expectation that good works would be an essential part of a person's faith and witness. Some Christians find it extraordinarily difficult to accept that one good deed could possibly exonerate a person for a lifetime of evil. Others are deeply sceptical, even a little queasy, about the whole notion of death-bed conversions, seeing it as a form of spiritual hedging of one's bets. Furthermore, there is the added complication that the name Penitent Thief appears to be somewhat of a misnomer, as there is no evidence in the Gospels of Dismas being penitent. This goes some way to explaining why there might be rather less emphasis on the role of the Good Thief in different Christian faith traditions. In some churches e.g. the Moravian Church, the Penitent Thief has no greater role, status, or significance than many of the other people that feature in the Bible. It remains the case that it is not uncommon for the Good Thief to receive scant attention,

---

68 The Oriental Orthodox Churches are composed of six autocephalus churches: the Armenian Apostolic Church, the Coptic Orthodox Church of Alexandria, the Eritrean Orthodox Tewahedo Church, the Ethiopian Orthodox Tewahedo Church, the Malankara Orthodox Syrian Church (Indian Orthodox Church) and the Syrian Orthodox Church of Antioch.

34 *The Penitent Thief* (1918) –
Francis Derwent Wood, Lady Lever
Art Gallery, Liverpool, UK.
This is an interesting portrayal of
Dismas, not least because the sculptor
had been a hospital volunteer during
the First World War and had worked
on the specialist of masks for soldiers
who had suffered severe facial
disfigurement. The Penitent Thief
featured here is older, careworn, and
portrayed with his mouth open.

**35 *Ivory carving of the
Crucifixion (Tenth Century)*** –
Walters Art Museum, Baltimore,
USA. A fine Byzantine carving
featuring a behaloed Christ with
the Virgin Mary and St. John the
Apostle. The event portrayed is
given added cosmic significance
by the presence
of a sun and moon.

36 *The Good Thief featured carrying his cross* in a Twelfth century mosaic
of the Last Judgement in the Basilica di Santa Maria Assunta, Torcello, Italy. This mosaic
of the Venetian-Byzantine school is one of the jewels of the Veneto.

38 *Le bon larron* (The Good Thief) Dismas (14th century)- Strasbourg Cathedral, France. Two soldiers are portrayed carrying out *crurifragium* (the breaking of legs) on Dismas and a baby-like soul is leaving his body and being received by an angel.

◁ **37 *The Crucifixion*** (circa 1310) - Duccio di Buoninsegna, Manchester Art Gallery, UK. There is still some debate as to the attribution of this painting, with Segna di Bonaventure and Ugolino di Nerio being suggested as alternatives. Mary Magdalene is clearly visible in red with her arms outstretched upwards in the direction of Jesus.

40 _The Crucifixion with the Virgin and Saint John the Evangelist Mourning_
(circa 1460) – Rogier van der Weyden, Philadelphia Museum of Art, Philadelphia, USA.
This masterpiece of the Northern Renaissance is a diptych. Simultaneously stark and
bold, its use of coloured cloth provides an extraordinary contrast that heightens the
presence of those individuals represented. It was painted in oil on oak panels.

◁ **39 _The Good Thief St. Dismas_** (circa 1455) – Unknown Spanish Master, National
Gallery of Denmark, Copenhagen. Dismas is shown dead on a Tau cross with both his
arms and legs cut. The bleak setting is heightened by having trees bare of leaves.

only seeming to warrant a fleeting mention during the services and readings of Holy Week. The Church of England does not recognise Dismas as a saint, although Jesus's exchange with him on the Cross is used, specifically Luke 23:43 (which *"may be softly repeated two or three times"*), as a suggested material of preparation when ministering to the dying.[69] In the Intercession Paper of the Guild of All Souls[70] the following prayers are offered as alternative weekly bidding prayers:

"We pray for all the dead. Jesus said to the penitent thief: 'Truly, I say to you, this day you will be with me in Paradise.' May these words be heard by all our departed brothers and sisters, especially ...."

"We pray for all who will die today, that they may hear those words of Christ, 'Today you will be with me in Paradise.'"

The story of the Good Thief is one of a number in the Scriptures that point to the central message of the Gospel, that through Jesus's sacrificial death on the Cross, our sins can be forgiven and we can rise with Him to eternal life. Be that as it may, the events of Holy Week, and especially the Paschal Triduum, are a constant challenge in respect of comprehension, our propensity to judge others, and of faith. Similarly, what the Irish poet and dramatist Aidan Mathews describes as; *"the dynamic double helix of death and resurrection"*[71] asks much of us. Study of the story of the Penitent Thief certainly raises plenty of questions for those concerned with soteriology.

---

69 Funeral – Ministry at the time of Death – Available at: https://www.churchofengland.org/prayer-and-worship/worship-texts-and-resources/common-worship/death-and-dying/funeral [Accessed 29 April 2020]

70 The Guild of All Souls is an Anglican devotional society.

71 Mathews, A. (2010). Good Thief, Bad Thief – two comments on Calvary. *The Furrow, 61*(4), p. 21.

A FATAL MISTAKE

Successive generations of clergy, theologians, Biblical scholars, and Christian believers have poured over Luke's account of the Penitent Thief's reaction to, and interaction with Jesus Christ on the Cross. For some there has been considerable doubt and perturbation, and dare I say it, soul-searching about the message that this encounter appears to send out to sinners. In a powerful sermon of 16th April 1699 entitled: *On the penitent thief* William Whiston[72] expressed his alarm at what he believed to be the misinterpretation of Luke 23:39–43. He posits that *"the mistake of this single text has perhaps been a great occasion of the ruin of more Christians than any other whatsoever in the whole Scripture".* He makes a spirited case which includes attempting to dismantle what he contemptuously calls *"bare Death-bed Repentance".* Whiston goes on to claim that there is no cast iron evidence that the Penitent Thief was impenitent to the last, that he might not have lead a life of total sin, and that the thief's initial doubting of the Messiah was more likely to be evidence of his own subscribing to the prevailing Orthodox Jewish attitude towards Jesus, that he was a blasphemer and spiritual mountebank.[73] The latter point is an interesting notion, that is impossible to verify. In respect of salvation, sin and a godly Christian life, the fact that the Lucan episode appears to fly in the face of all other Biblical teaching is espoused by Whiston, who was convinced that; *"a Fatal Mistake has been committed; and that the text has been sadly misunderstood hitherto and this for the Unhappy Ruin of many thousand souls for ever."* The *"Fatal Mistake"* in his opinion being that

---

72 William Whiston (1667–1752) was a notable English theologian, historian, and mathematician. Whiston, W. (1709), 'On the penitent thief', in *Sermons and essays upon several subjects.* B. Took, London, pp. 5–27.

73 Implicit in such reasoning is that the Penitent Thief was a Jew, something that is decidedly at odds with the notion that Dismas was a Gentile, possibly an Egyptian.

the sinful wrongly believe that a sudden *"bare Death-bed repentance"* would be enough to wipe the slate clean and ensure their salvation. Some Christians continue to be troubled lest this Gospel story be used as a licence for sin. In sermons of this nature a perennial preoccupation is that of a person having lived a godly Christian life.

Thomas Newman's[74] *The case of the thief on the cross considered as made an encouragment to a death-bed repentance* (1751)[75] offers a cogent and masterly dissection of any argument that purports to claim that the example of what happened to the Penitent Thief can be used as the reason or excuse for death-bed repentance. His antipathy to such eleventh hour repentance is made apparent early on in the treatise: *"This appears to me a most deadly engine for the destruction of souls; a most fatal opiate; a wretched strategem to unite and reconcile the wildest extremes of moral character and condition; even those of indulgence to wickedness and the hopes of salvation; a living to the Devil and a dying to the Lord."* Newman is deeply sceptical about such a belief, seeing it as a negation of Gospel teaching, one that in modern parlance is akin to moral hazard. He asks why if all that were needed for salvation is a death-bed repentance, was it not mentioned elsewhere in Scripture? The fact that as a rule we do not choose the time or manner of our death adds to the danger, one of eternal damnation. He also makes the point that the Penitent Thief did not sin presuming later mercy or in depending on late or death-bed repentance, yet others believing in such a route, sin because they believe that they have a means to absolve themselves at such a time as they are unable to sin any more.

---

74 Thomas Newman (1692–1758) was a Dissenting Minister at the Carter Lane Meeting House, Blackfriars, London.

75 Newman, T. (1751), *The case of the thief on the cross considered, as made an encouragement to a death-bed repentance.* R. Hett & J. Waugh, London.

In reflecting on the Penitent Thief's conduct Newman discerns that in the exceptional circumstances of the Crucifixion, where Dismas not only had a privileged vantage point, but shared the physical pain of Jesus, his behaviour was exceptional. For all the fact that he might have imbibed the prejudices against the Nazarene, Newman makes an original suggestion when he observes of the thief that; *"he is so far from appearing a late penitent, that in reality, his situation being considered, he was an early convert;"*. This certainly provides food for thought in the light of fact that he perceived evidence for the Good Thief's assurance of salvation in the extraordinary condition in which Jesus Christ was being put to death; *"I apprehend it was this illustrious and singular testimony bore to the blessed Jesus, at so peculiar a season, when his circumstances conspired to discourage all faith, hope and trust in him, that was the ground of that favour and assurance of acceptance that he received from our Lord. Herein this dying criminal exceeded the Apostles themselves."* This is instructive and gives further reason to look at the Good Thief and his significance anew.

One of the most insightful and moving sermons that has survived from the Eighteenth Century is one delivered by Andrew Eliot D.D.[76] a church minister in Boston, Massachusettes, America. What makes this sermon all the more remarkable is that its subject *Christ's promise to the penitent thief* was requested by Levi Ames, a prisoner, present at the service, who had been sentenced to death for burglary, and was to die less than a week later on 21st October 1773. Eliot in expounding on the Penitent Thief's conversation with Jesus declares; *"We scarce find such an instance of faith in the whole book of God!"* He like others ponders on whether Dismas had any prior knowledge of Jesus and his

76 Eliot, A. (1773), *Christ's Promise to the Penitent Thief.* John Boyle, Boston.

earthly ministry. Unsurprisingly, Eliot's congregation is reminded of the meaning of Paradise and are informed that in respect of the Penitent Thief that; *"Our lord knew the change which divine grace had wrought in him."* Interestingly there are echoes of Thomas Newman's concern about the danger of death-bed repentance, although Eliot declares that; *"none need to despair, but all ought to repair to his merciful High Priest,"* – the High Priest referred to being Jesus Christ. The sermon is a veritable clarion call to repentance and prayer, with the following line being especially salient; *"Repentance, when true, is never too late, and therefore the thief upon the cross is a sovereign antidote against despair."* Out of the humiliation and ignominy of his Crucifixion Christ triumphs again emerging with the Penitent Thief as an *"illustrious trophy of divine power and grace."*

To the thief in the congregation Eliot reminds the *"poor unhappy youth"* (his youth is mentioned several times; he was 21 years of age) that he is *"within the reach of mercy".* He also addresses Levi Ames directly as; *"You, my friend...".* The parallels between the two thieves would not have been lost on the congregation, nor mention of *"Christ interceding for sinners in the court of heaven."* Jesus being the route to Salvation ensures that we can all appreciate the following line directed at the burglar in a Boston church; *"Commit this inestimable treasure, your precious and immortal spirit, into his hands,".*

Ames went to the gallows for his crime and addressed the assembled throng with the following words prior to his execution as recorded by Samuel Stilmann:

"Look at me, a sight enough to melt a heart of stone; I am going to die for my wickedness: But the death I am to die, is nothing compared with the death of JESUS CHRIST on the cross, for they pierced his hands and his side with a spear. O take warning by me—If you were my own brethren, near

to me as my own soul, I could only tell you to beware of stealing, swearing, [and] drinking."[77]

Levi Ames could be said to have been a penitent thief.

Both Dismas and Levi Ames had transgressed and made a fatal mistake that had brought them to earthly justice, yet none of us, whether a convicted criminal or not, can afford to neglect matters appertaining to the soul and divine justice.

THE PENITENT THIEF
AND THE JOURNEY OF FAITH

In any exploration of the life, meaning and example of the Good Thief there needs to be an appreciation that his conduct elicits different reactions and that these can be both polarised and nuanced. St. Augustine of Hippo, whilst not naming the Penitent Thief mused on whether he was baptised at some point. Others too have discussed whether baptism is necessary for salvation as Dismas was not baptised. For some theologians, his death with Jesus Christ became his baptism, his soul washed by suffering and repentance with the Blood of Christ, his being a witness to the Supreme Sacrifice for Mankind. There is a debate to be had in some quarters as to how the Penitent Thief managed to bypass purgatory, accepting of course that not all Christian denominations believe in the existence of purgatory. Some Christian believers have been perplexed by Dismas's privileged status as one who was translated to the heavenly kingdom despite a life of sin. In both the Orthodox and Catholic churches the extraordinary promise made to the Penitent Thief by the Messiah and recorded in

77 Stilmann, S (1808). The Character of a Foolish Son. In *Samuel Stilmann Selected Sermons on Doctrinal and Practical Subjects* (pp.191–231). Maning and Loring. Boston.

41 *Crucifixion /Antwerpen Crucifixion* (1475) – Antonello de Messina, Royal
Museum of Fine Arts, Antwerp, Belgium. A sparing and deftly handled work that in
common with other Crucifixion scenes features the Virgin Mary and St. John
the Evangelist. Note the owl in the foreground, a bird replete with meanings, some
to do with darkness and death, yet in Crucifixion scenes they are believed to be
a symbol of Redemption.

42 ***Passion of Christ fresco*** (circa 1491), Giovanni Canavesio, Notre Dame de Fontaine Chapelle, La Brigue, France. Dismas is clearly shown on Jesus's right where he is being finished off by soldiers. In the bottom left-hand corner of the fresco the Virgin Mary is shown overcome with grief, whilst in the bottom right a dispute over the division of Jesus's garments results in soldiers coming to blows.

43 *Passion of Christ fresco* (circa 1491) featuring the Harrowing of Hell, Giovanni Canavesio, Notre Dame de Fontaine Chapelle, La Brigue, France. An extremely youthful looking Dismas (clearly marked Dimas) is portrayed accompanying Christ on his triumphant decent into Hell to rescue the Righteous.

△ **44** *St. Dismas stained glass* (circa 1539) – Church of Saint-Yves, La Roche-Maurice, Brittany, France. This masterly work in common with many other portrayals of the Crucifixion in showing the thieves tied rather than nailed to a cross, this is almost certainly an error that has been repeated down the centuries. Both Dismas and the Virgin Mary would be to Christ's right and this is enormously significant.

45 *Detail of Dismas* – The Good Thief in a Sixteenth Century stained glass window located in the Chapel of St. Martin in the Catholic Church of Saint Pierre, Dreux, The Loire Valley, France. Note the childlike soul of the Good Thief being received by an angel. Photograph by G. Freihalter.

46 *The Crucifixion of Christ* (16th century) – Hans Speckaert, Metroplitan Museum of Art, New York, USA. A deeply sensitive piece that features heavenly light behind the figure of Christ. The Good Thief is visible, whilst the Bad Thief is largely hidden. Here we see an example of what is often called the Swoon of the Virgin Mary, known as *Lo Spasimo*.

47 *Dimas, el Buen Ladrón (The Good Thief)*, from the Sixth Anguish of the Virgin Mary by Gregorio Fernández (circa 1616), National Museum of Sculpture, Valladolid, Spain. In Spanish St. Dismas is called San Dimas and has been a familiar figure in processions held to mark the Passion of Christ. This sculpture portrays the Sixth Sorrow of Mary: The Crucifixion and the Descent from the Cross.

48 *The Crucifixion* (1711) – Ionnis Moskos, Digitized Archive of the Hellenic Institute of Venice, Italy. The Wise Robber is turned towards Christ and making his famed request; *"Remember me, Lord in your Kingdom."* The Romans and Jews hostile to Jesus are portrayed with decidedly Turkish looking features and attire reflecting the prevailing antipathy in Christendom at the time this work was created.

49 An altar painting of der Gute Schächer (the Good Thief) looking youthful and seemingly carefree by Joseph Karpf (1733) in the Catholic Church of the Visitation of the Virgin Mary, Gottmannshofen, Bavaria, Germany. Photograph by G. Freihalter

50 Statue of St. Dismas (1750) on a bridge in Březnice, Příbram district, Czech Republic. Central Bohemia has long had a devotion to St. Dismas. The fine statuary on this bridge over the River Skalice echoes in style the type of devotional statues to be found on the Charles Bridge, that crosses the Vltava River in Prague.

93

Luke 23:43 has meant that he has never been formally canonized, but is revered as a Saint nonetheless by virtue of the special nature of his encounter with Jesus on the Cross.

Some uncertainty continues to surround his life and name, and this can feed doubts as to the veracity of accounts such as the story expounded on by St. Anselm. The Arabian Gospel of Christs's childhood (*Syriac Infancy Gospel*), a deuterocanonical book, believed to date from the 5th or 6th century AD refers to a severe briggand Dumah and a merciful one as Tyth. The 6th–7th century Evangelion (Gospel Book) *Codex Usserianus Primus*, whilst partially lost, names one of the thieves, believed to be the obstinate one, Capnatas. The 7th–8th century *Codex Rehdigeranus* calls them Ioatha and Maggatras.[78] Equally the 11th Century *Codex Colbertinus* mentions Zoatham (The Good Thief) and Camma (The Bad Thief), thus there is potential for confusion and occasional poetic licence. Mistranslation of, and interpolation in various texts over the centuries has muddied the waters and caused some to question. That said, the Penitent Thief has become a symbol of hope, especially for prisoners and others whose lives may have fallen well short of the ideal. Dismas (or Dimas in Portuguese and Spanish) and the juxtaposition of good and evil that is synonymous with the events of the Crucifixion are a powerful reminder that it is only through Christ that salvation can be achieved. Pope Francis in a General Audience of 28th September 2016 chose to give an address entitled *Forgiveness on the Cross* in which he made a direct reference to St. Dismas:

"His words are a wonderful example of repentance, a catechesis centred on learning to ask Jesus for forgiveness."

---

78 On some textual variants in the Gospels – Available at: https://forums.catholic.com/t/on-some-textual-variants-in-the-gospels/326833/46 [Accessed 17 April 2020]

Significantly, the Pontiff goes on to refer to *"the fear of God. Not the dread of God,".*[79]

Dismas's acknowledgement of the kingly power of Jesus Christ means that he is frequently the subject of Gospel readings (taken from Luke 23:35–43) and homilies during the Feast of Christ the King.[80] The Catholic, Anglican and Lutheran Churches among others observe this feast and by so doing explore and reflect upon the sovereignty of Christ.

John Calvin (1509–1564), the French theologian and reformer, is another who set considerable store by the Penitent Thief, seeing his acknowledgement of Jesus as an act of faith and repentance, one that directly resulted in his own salvation. Calvin's seminal work *Institutes of the Christian Religion* (1536) offers a Reformist interpretation of Luke's account of Christ's promise to the Penitent Thief and uses the passage to justify the doctrine of election/predestination. Dwelling on the Good Thief's acceptance of his own sin and his confession of the innocence of Christ we would do well to remember those words from the Book of Proverbs: *"He who conceals his transgressions will not prosper, but he who confesses and foresakes them will obtain mercy."* (Proverbs 28:13). Dismas remains a figure who can serve to remind us of our own failings and transgressions and of the centrality of acknowledging our sins, showing contrition, and accepting that by having faith in Jesus Christ we receive God's grace.

---

79 Pope Francis General Audience Wednesday 28 September 2016 – Available at: www.vatican.va/content/francesco/en/audiences/2016/documents/papa-francesco_20160928_udienza-generale.html [Accessed 28 March 2020]

80 Pope Pius XI instituted the Solemnity of Our Lord Jesus Christ, King of the Universe, more commonly known as the Feast of Christ the King or Christ the King Sunday, in 1925 with his encyclical *Quas Primus* (In the first) to respond to growing nationalism and secularism.

There is something to be gained from reflecting on the fact that as far as we know Jesus was largely taciturn during his interviews and interrogations by Ciaphas and the Sanhedrin, Pontius Pilate, and Herod Antipas, yet when Dismas made his petition to him on the Cross he immediately responded. Jesus had been silent, except for a brief request to His father, when the assembled throng at Golgotha had abused and chastised him but readily answered the Good Thief's entreaty in the affirmative. At that moment Dismas was no longer an extra in this tragic scene, he became a focus of supreme love and thereby an example and hope for all who recognise and admit their own sinfulness, whilst being prepared to accept and acknowledge the supremacy of Christ.

Charles Kingsley (1819–1875), an Anglican clergyman, in a sermon on the theme of the Penitent Thief asserts that; *"The story of the penitent thief is a most beautiful and affecting one. Christians' hearts in all times, have clung to it for comfort, not only for themselves, but for those whom they loved."*[81] Maybe this should set us thinking not only about ourselves and those we love or have loved, but also about those who, for whatever reason, are without love or are themselves unloved, or feel unloved or believe that they are beyond the reach of God's love.

DISMAS AND PRISON MINISTRY

Dismas is held, albeit unofficially, to be the Patron Saint of Prisoners[82] (especially the condemned), Prison Chaplains, Penitent Sinners and Undertakers. Several commentators have observed that Dismas is

---

81 Charles Kingsley Sermon XXXI, The Penitent Thief – Available at: www.online-literature.com/charles-kingsley/the-good-news/31/ [Accessed 1 May 2020]

82 St. Leonard has often been invoked by prisoners, although in more recent years in the Catholic Church St. Maximilian Kolbe (1894–1941) has been designated the Patron Saint of Prisoners.

the patron of those who have engaged in dishonest business and would like to make restitution before they die, but do not know how. Those engaging in sharp or dishonest practice is likely to be quite a sizeable group, but how many are prepared to change and have the courage to publicly acknowledge their wrongdoing? His name is especially associated with those who are involved with prison ministry and efforts to engage in the rehabilitation of prisoners. Society at large takes a very dim view of those in prison and young offender institutions, and often has precious little sympathy for those whose crimes, alleged or otherwise, have resulted in their loss of liberty. Whilst like Dismas there are those who have lived lives of sin and transgression, his example reminds us that even those that need to face up to what they have done deserve an opportunity to mend their ways and seek salvation. We often forget that some prisoners are in prison on remand and then there are those who are the victims of grave miscarriages of justice, anyone familiar with the case of Stefan Kisko (1952–1993) will appreciate that those found guilty of a crime are sometimes innocent. Justice and penal systems the world over are like humanity, often deeply flawed.

St. Dismas is not the only saint with a disreputable past, St. Moses the Abyssinian (330–405 AD), St. Mary of Egypt (344–421 AD), St. Augustine (354–430 AD) and St Angela of Foligno (1248–1309) all transgressed yet managed to redeem themselves. In the Penitent Thief we have someone who stands as a supreme example of one who even in the moment of his utter degradation recognised the majesty of Christ and in humility acknowledged his own wrong-doing and asked to be remembered. Across the world there are prison ministries that demonstrate that prisoners and ex-prisoners are not only not forgotten, they are deemed worthy of mission, support, and prayer.

Many of these Christian ministries have chosen to operate with Dismas's name and example front and centre of their work.

In America and further afield there are prison and penitentiary churches and chapels dedicated to the Penitent Thief, an example being the Church of St. Dismas, The Good Thief, in the grounds of Clinton County Correctional Facility, Dannemora in upstate New York, whilst in the Philippines there is a chapel dedicated to Saint Dimas at Manila City Jail. The example of the Penitent Thief has inspired Christian outreach programmes of different denominations dedicated to bringing the Word and Christian love to those whom society has incarcerated. Since the late 1950s and early 1960s atttitudes to prison outreach and ministry[83] has been more understanding and proactive, with the likes of the Diocese of Pennsylvania, USA launching the Episcopal Fellowship of St. Dismas at Holmesburg Prison, an organisation of clergy and lay people ministering to inmates and former prisoners using trained supporters known as "outmates".[84] Over the years ventures of this nature have waxed and waned, but the need has remained, if anything it has grown. Enlightened initiatives such as the opening of two San Dimas Centers for the Pastoral Care of Prisons by the Catholic Archdiocese of Miami's Prison Ministry[85] are helping change attitudes and support prisoners, ex-prisoners, and high-risk youths. Whilst invariably every effort is made to reach out and support all without prejudice or judgement, there is always the wish, and the hope that inmates and ex-offenders might choose to take a spiritual path, one where they grow to know Jesus Christ. In the

83 It is sometimes known as Detention Ministry.
84 'Pennsylvania – Church Ministers to Prisoners', 12 December 1965, *The Living Church*, The Episcopal Church, p. 6.
85 Miami, Florida, USA is a majority Latino city, with approximately 70% of the population being of Hispanic heritage, thus the name San Dimas is used rather than Saint Dismas.

words of Dietrich Bonhoeffer,[86] someone who was only too familiar with what it was like to be incarcerated; *"Jesus himself did not try to convert the two thieves on the cross, he waited until one of them turned to him."*

Dismas is commonly and quite deliberately chosen as the patron or name of these outreach and prison ministry programmes, for he is a symbol of hope for those who normally might be without hope. St. Dismas Orthodox Prison Ministry, a labour of love of St. Nicholas Orthodox Church, Fletcher, North Carolina, USA is typical of those outreach programmes that believe that such work and mission is the duty of the Church, whilst demonstrating a concern and compassion for those who often feel forgotten and unloved. Its founder and volunteer Mary-Jo Dukas (aka Mama-Jo) explains their work with prisoners thus:

"Firstly, we extend a hand of friendship with no strings attached. Our communication is honest, informative and personalized. We don't try to "save people", but rather to be a friend and someone to talk to.

We offer a different perspective, historical and theological, that awakens hope and curiosity in people. We reiterate that Christ came to save everyone— not just a predetermined group. We stress that it is our job to do the work—to claim that salvation and cling to it. We stand on historical facts and the firm footing of Orthodox Christian Theology and Holy Tradition.

We ask our participants to pray for us and for certain situations and bring them into a family with friends inside and outside of prison. Our goal is to create a sense of belonging, purpose and hope."

---

86 Dietrich Bonhoeffer (1906–1945) was a German Lutheran pastor, theologian, and anti-Nazi dissident. The quotation is taken from: *Dietrich Bonhoeffer – Letter and Papers from Prison* (Originally published in 1951).

Some places of worship have even been built, or partially constructed by prisoners such as the Church of the Good Thief, Kingston, Ontario, Canada which was built with limestone quarried, cut and transported by prisoners from Kingston Penitenitiary, and *La Chiesa de Boun Ladrone* (The Church of the Penitent Thief), Frazione di La Mura San Carlo, San Lazzaro di Savera, Bologna, Italy[87] where prisoners coming towards the end of their sentences received skills training in construction as part of their rehabilitation.[88]

In France there is *La Fraternité du Bon Larron* (The Brotherhood of the Good Thief) that works assiduously to provide inmates and those leaving prison with fraternal and spiritual support. The Churches of Christ in Victoria and Tasmania, Australia (a movement of approximately 130 churches and agencies) has in the Friends of Dismas a church for parolees, ex-prisoners, and their family and friends that seeks: *"to assist motivated adults on parole, ex-prisoners, and their family and friends, to grow in Christian faith, to transition successfully into society, and to live a crime free life."*[89] In Thessalonica, Greece the Diaconary for the Release of Poor Prisoners and Defendants does important, some might say liberating work, that is constantly inspired by St. Xenia of Rome and the Holy Thief of Golgotha. Whilst in California, USA the Brotherhood of St. Dismas takes as its focus prayer, penance, and charity, with its outreach being especially directed to those who have

---

87   In Italy the thieves are called Disma (The Good Thief) and Misma (The Bad Thief). The Church of St. Francis of Assisi in Gallipoli, Apulia is known locally as *La Chiesa de Malladrone* (The Church of the Bad Thief) as it contains a grinning and malevolent carving of Misma that appears to attract rather more attention than the one of Disma.

88   *The Church of the Penitent Thief*, CHB journal, 20 October 2019 – Available at: www.churchbuilding.co.uk/church-penitent-thief/ [Accessed 7 April 2020]

89   Churches of Christ in Victoria and Tasmania – Friends of Dismas Available at: www.churchesofchrist.org.au/communities/neighbourhood-engagement/careworks/friends-of-dismas [Accessed 4 April 2020]

been in prison or have been involved in gangs, or drugs. A primary focus of the work with former prison inmates is to significantly reduce rates of recidivism. In some countries the name Dismas is synonymous with homes, hostels, drugs rehabilitation units and projects supporting and upliting others.

Not every organisation bearing the name of the Good Thief has a religious purpose, but all seek to value and enrich lives. Jeff Backus, House Director of Hartford Dismas House[90] (Dismas of Vermont Inc) speaks with conviction when he declares that *"the spirit of St. Dismas is alive and well through our mission identifying that individuals are so much more than their worst moment."*. In various Dismas associated initiatives staff and teams of volunteers reach out in a manner that is both humbling and inspiring. So much of the work being done involves finding majesty in the margins, and helping individuals become the people that they want to be, rather than define them by the person they once were. Dismas House of Vermont exemplifies those organisations that do not seek to proselytise residents; yet are determined to look for the good in others and create safe and supportive environments where people are empowered and enabled to change. Having *"a mission to reconcile prisoners to society and society to prisoners"* requires a spirit of reconciliation, something that is desperately needed in our fractured and judgemental world. Rita Whalen McCaffrey, Founder of Dismas of Vermont, which has four Vermont Dismas Houses, sums up its work

90 The first Dismas House was established in St. Louis in 1959 by Fr. Charles 'Dismas' Clark, a Jesuit priest, with the help of Maurice Shenker, a defense attorney, as a halfway house to support men coming out of prison. The initiative proved to be a remarkable success and something of its story was told in the film *The Hoodlum Priest* (1961) by Irvin Kershner. Further such houses were opened across America, and the idea emulated both locally and internationally. The following academic paper makes interesting reading; Werner, S. (2016). [About the Cover]: Frank Sinatra and the Hoodlum Priest. *American Catholic Studies, 127*(4), pp. 101–108.

as follows; *"Dismas is a change agent for former prisoners and a change agent for the community of staff and volunteers. Former prisoners yearn 'to be accepted for what they are now' and not anymore as the 'criminal they once were.' Our program model allows the community to experience Dismas residents as human beings, helping the prisoners' self image from that of 'born to lose' to 'you are accepted'."* This message of acceptance and hope speaks volumes of how the Dismas story continues to inspire and transform lives in diverse ways.

LEARNING TO LOOK AS WELL AS SEE

The oldest known extant church dedicated to the Good Thief is that of the Chapel of St. Dismas (1706) in Zagreb (formerly Agram), Croatia, where in earlier times prisoners awaiting execution at the nearby North Gate could repent of their sins. The final hours of the Penitent Thief's life caused him to confront his own sin, to accept his wrongdoing, and to show humility when others might have railed against God and the world. He did not ask to be freed or fast-tracked to Heaven, he simply asked that Jesus remember him. In our own lives we are often in denial about our own imperfections; our lives are dominated by pride and conceit and all too often we abdicate responsibility for our actions and seek to blame others, including God himself. Some are guilty of heinous crimes, of blasphemies and actions that warrant serious censure. Many, if not all of us, think ignoble thoughts, lie to others, lie to ourselves and seek to lie to God. We are ever ready to accuse others, to engage in *schadenfreude*, and spread gossip in a manner that does untold damage. There is much that we can learn from those profound words spoken by Iago to Othello in Act III Scene III of the play *Othello* by William Shakespeare (1564–1616):

51 Church of Saint Dismas in the village of Dříteň, České Budějovice District, Czech Republic. In view of the dedication of this church and its location in Bohemia it might well be a suitable setting for a recital of the music of the celebrated Bohemian composer Jan Dismas Zelenka (1679–1745).

52 Statue of San Dimas in the Basilica de Nuestra Señora de Zapopan (Basilica of Our Lady of Zapopan), Jalisco, Mexico. Both the Spanish and the Portuguese took a reverence of San Dimas with them to the New World and further afield. Here San Dimas is behaloed and looking left in the direction of Christ.

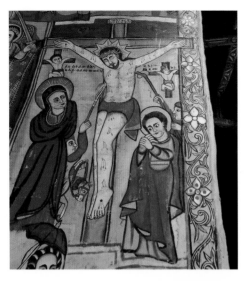

53 Wall painting in Ura Kidane Mihret, an Ethiopian Orthodox Church on the Zege Peninsula, on the southern shores of Lake Tana, Ethiopia. This striking portrayal of the Crucifixion scene gives prominence to Jesus and the Virgin Mary, whilst also featuring the Good Thief making his request to Jesus. Unlike some Western artists this work does not shy away from showing that Christ has been thoroughly scourged.

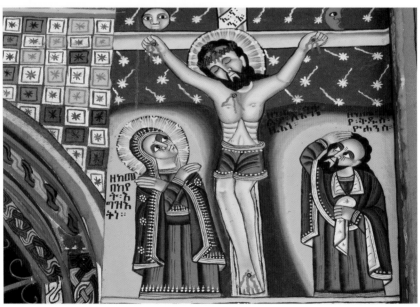

54 Crucifixion scene painted on the façade of the I Yesus Church, Axum (Aksum), Tigray Region, Ethiopia. A universal theme in depictions of the Crucifixion is the emphasis on the heavens, especially the sun and moon. Civilisations have often had a keen sense of cosmic influences and thus it is important that we take note of such portrayals and their significance.

55 *The Crucifixion by the Romans* (1887) – Vasily Vereshchagin, Private Collection. A crucifixion was meant to be seen and this painting by an eminent Russian war artist places the viewer firmly among the spectators. Historians and Biblical scholars continue to argue as to the precise location of Golgotha, but there is a general agreement that it was near to Jerusalem, with many believing that Jesus and the two thieves were crucified facing west.

56 _Crucifixion with Darkened Sun_ (1907) – Egon Schiele, Private Collection. This
Expressionist piece takes the viewer on a journey into suffering symbolism. The eye
is drawn towards Christ and the Good Thief, although there is a realisation that this
is a time of immense agony. The sun is eclipsed whilst the Son of Man is adorned with
a golden halo. It is incredible to think that the artist was only seventeen years old when
he painted this.

57 *Calvary* (1926) –
Alfred Frank Hardiman,
Old St. Paul's Church,
Edinburgh, UK. This stylised
and beautifully executed
work reveals the influence
of Etruscan and Classical
Roman sculpture. Like many
works of art, it has made
the mistake of portraying
Christ with his feet
overlayed, rather than nailed
individually.

58 *Christ Head* (1952) – Alexis
Preller, Iziko South African National
Gallery, Cape Town, South Africa. This
work of oil and wood reflects European
and African influences. Masks and their
association with the spirit of the soul
raises interesting questions about how
we perceive, portray, and interpret
Christ and the Crucifixion.

"Good name in man and woman, dear my lord,
Is the immediate jewel of their souls.
Who steals my purse steals trash; 'Tis something, nothing:
'Twas mine, 'tis his, and has been slave to thousands.
But he that filches from me my good name
Robs me of that which not enriches him
And makes me poor indeed."[91]

Like Dismas we too live lives of sin and would do well to grant ourselves manumission from that enslavement that diminishes and corrupts our lives and that of others. Our addiction to exploiting, traducing, or belittling our fellow human beings, or to conspicuous consumption, to alcohol, recreational drugs, pornography etc. is a reminder of our own failings and raises legitimate questions about whether we are really fit to point the finger and sit in judgment on others. Sadly, many supposed believers are censorious, sanctimonious, and lacking in charity. There is a need to be watchful of falling into an arid and routine Christianity that is devoid of humility and love for those that society marginalises, ignores, or seeks to despise and condemn. All too often we permit Confirmation Bias to dominate our dealings with others, metaphorically speaking we allow ourselves to become judge, jury, and executioner. We expect clemency and forgiveness for ourselves, but routinely deny it to others. We would all do well to remember that a person's past, and that includes prisoners and ex-offenders, does not have to dictate his or her future. Equally, it is good to be reminded of the fact that no one is beyond God's reach. The Penitent Thief stands as a symbol of the Lord's Divine Mercy.

---

91 The Complete Works of William Shakespeare – Available at: http://shakespeare.mit.edu/ othello/othello.3.3.html [Accessed 2 April 2020]

59 *Chapel of St. Dismas* (1706), Zagreb, Croatia. As in former times prisoners passed this chapel en route to their execution there might have been an element of it providing some consolation and reminding them that it is never too late to turn to Christ. Nowadays this small chapel is known for having in its possession the sandals of a modern saint – St. Theresa of Calcutta.

It is not for me to engage in asseveration as to Dismas's status as a saint, suffice it to say that in some churches he is viewed as one, whilst by others he is not. What is not in dispute is the role that he plays during the Crucifixion and the fact that his wonderous discernment brings about a miraculous transformation. A life sullied by sin undergoes a transfiguration. Faith, hope, and yes indeed charity coalesce and transmute one with a dark heart into someone who is compassionate, even loving. The Penitent Thief serves as a reminder of the role of personal sin and salvation – *"these traditional anvils of Christian theology."*[92]

Out of the darkness and degradation of the Crucifixion comes a remarkable luminous clarity in the words and actions of Dismas. Whilst the Good Thief had initially reviled Christ, he sees the error of his ways and essentially repents. He recognises and acknowledges the innocence and sovereignty of Jesus of Nazareth and rebukes Gestas about their own guilt. At a time when his movement was severely restricted, whether he be bound or adhered to or nailed to the cross,[93] he liberates himself as never before and is freed from the slavery of his sinful past. His courage and honesty readies him for Salvation, something that some find difficult to fathom. It is hard to imagine what Dismas might have been thinking in those final hours that he lived on earth after the death of Jesus Christ. Whether he was confident and serene in those last hours is a matter of conjecture, but at his nadir in execution he had reached the zenith of Salvation, for in asking to be remembered he was assured of so much more than that: *"Truly, I say to*

92 Krieg, C. (1973). Bonhoeffer's Letters and Papers. *Religious Studies, 9*(1), p.82
93 Artists often erroneously portray the thieves as having been bound to the cross, whilst all the evidence of crucifixion in the Ancient World points to them having been nailed rather than tied.

you, today you will be with me in Paradise." (Luke 23:43). To receive such a reply from He that is the Prince of Peace and the Light of the World must have been the sweetest balm at a time of pain and torment.

Yet our tendency is to doubt and question. We find ourselves wondering what the Penitent Thief felt like when Jesus died. We know from the Gospel accounts that the thieves lived on for several hours more; many in his position would feel abandoned, desolate, and utterly without hope. He endured until he finally breathed his last. What then? Is it true? How do we know? What happened to his body? Questions flood in, as they always do. Our own faith is often uncertain, for like Thomas the Apostle we have our doubts and will not believe until we have seen and touched the wounds. How would we have reacted had we been at the Crucifixion, would we have stood at a distance, filled with fear and apprehension lest someone identify us as a follower of the Nazarene? Might we be one of those happy to chastise the condemned in the knowledge that our own conduct is often less than worthy? Maybe we would try to comfort some of the family and friends of those on the cross. Or would we be looking on in ghoulish fascination, eager to tell others of what we had seen? Thankfully in 33AD selfies and social media did not exist, but that would not have stopped some taking a perverse delight in telling others of what they had witnessed and recounting gruesome details with relish. Hopefully, we would have offered up a prayer and wished for the suffering to be over quickly. To believers the mocking crowd on that day seems emblematic of the whole world, one that had rejected the Son of Man and was content to see him bloodied, broken and reviled. In such a hostile situation, how do we know that our courage would not fail us? Might we like Simon Peter, deny knowledge of Christ, or as some do in their daily life push belief and worship to the margins or leave observance to a Sunday or to certain religious festivals? Is our Christian faith to be put on and taken off as the mood or situation requires it? Are we fair-weather Christians fearful of that which might demand more of us?

We can safely assume that Dismas knew nothing of what was to come, of a splintered church, of dogma, and of doctrinal and denominational discord. For all his manifest sins he managed to look as well as see, and in the Passion of Jesus recognised the Divinity of Christ. He remains someone who has lessons to teach each one of us on our quest for moral and spiritual transformation. Dismas is so much more than a bit player in the Crucifixion. Let not our habitual failings be an impediment to our desire to be both better people and genuine believers. The Penitent Thief can serve as a reminder of just how far we can journey, even though there is much that is beyond our mortal comprehension. Maybe in reflecting on the story and example of the Good Thief we will gain a clearer understanding of what it is to acknowledge Jesus Christ and his centrality to our Salvation. On earth we may wish to see before we believe, but like Dismas, to be assured of a place in heaven, it is through believing that we will truly see.

60 *St. Dismas on one of the Deacon's Doors*, St. Nicholas Orthodox Church, Fletcher, North Carolina, USA – Photograph by Mary-Jo Dukas. The Deacon's Doors – the two doors at the north and south end of the iconostasis leading into the sanctuary, which represents heaven. To quote Mary-Jo Dukas; *"He* (St. Dismas) *is the one who greets us as we approach the gates of Paradise! Imagine that!"*

113

GLOSSARY

Amharic – is a Semitic language that is the official language of Ethiopia

Aramaic – is a Semitic language which was the lingua franca of much of the Near East from about 7th century BC until the 7th century AD, when it was largely superseded by Arabic

apse – a semicircular recess in a church that is covered with a hemispherical vault or semi-dome

Atonement – the reconciliation of God and mankind through Jesus Christ

autocephalus – is the status of a hierarchical Christian church whose head bishop does not report to any higher-ranking bishop

beatific – feeling or expressing blissful happiness, imparting holy bliss

Canonical Gospels – are the first four books of the New Testament; the Gospels of Matthew, Mark, Luke and John narrate the life, death and resurrection of Jesus

catechesis – religious instruction

Cinquecento – the collective name for the cultural and artistic events of Italy during the period 1500 to 1599

Confirmation Bias – is a type of cognitive bias that involves favouring information that confirms your previously existing beliefs, biases or prejudices

deuterocanonical – (of sacred books or literary works) forming a secondary canon

dramaturgy – is the study of dramatic composition and the representation of the main elements of drama on the stage.

eschatalogical – relating to death, judgement, and the final destiny of the soul and of humankind

expiation – the act of making amends or reparation for guilt or wrongdoing

funambulism – tightrope walking

hagiology – literature dealing with the lives and legends of saints

iconostasis – is a screen or wall of icons and religious paintings, seperating the nave from the sanctuary in a church (in Eastern Christianity)

manumission – release from slavery

Mariology – is the theological study of the Virgin Mary, the mother of Jesus

mediatrix – refers to the intercessory role of the Virgin Mary, the mother of Jesus

monotheistic – characterized or relating to the belief that there is only one God

nimbus – a halo or circle of light surrounding a person in a work of art

Parasceve – the day of preparation before the Jewish Sabbath

Paschal – relating to Easter; it can also be used to relate to the Jewish Passover

pathetic fallacy – the atttribution of human emotions to inanimate things, especially in art or literature

Pax Romana – Roman Peace

pericope – an extract from a text, especially a passage from the Bible

philologist – a person who studies literary texts

polytheistic – characterized or relating to a belief in more than one god

proper – the part of a church service that varies with the feast or season

recidivism – the tendency of a convicted criminal to reoffend

sacerdotal – relating to priests and the priesthood; priestly

Sanhedrin – the supreme council and tribunal of the Jews in ancient times

schadenfreude – a German word that means the pleasure derived by someone from another person's misfortune

Soteriology – the doctrine of salvation

toponymists – people who study place names

Triduum – a religious observance lasting three days

Zealot – a member of a Jewish political movement called The Zealots which in ancient times sought to incite the people of Judaea to rebel against Roman rule

WEBSITES WITH A DISMAS CONNECTION

Comunidad San Dimas | www.comunidadsandimas.org/saint_dismas
Dismas Charities Inc | www.dismas.com/
Dismas Fellowship Network | http://dismasfellowshipnetwork.com/
Dismas Home – New Hampshire | www.dismashomenh.org
Dismas House of St. Louis | www.dismashouse.net/
Dismas House – Worcester & Oakham | www.dismasisfamily.org/
Dismas/Magdalene Project | www.dismag.org
Dismas Ministry – A National Catholic Prison Outreach |
   https://dismasministry.org/
Dismas of Vermont | https://dismasofvt.org/
Friends of Dismas | www.friendsofdismas.com/
La Fraternité du Bon Larron | http://bonlarron.org/ (In French)
Society of St. Dismas | http://stdismas.com/
St. Didacus Church – Brotherhood of St. Dismas | www.stdidacus.org/112
St. Dismas Archives | http://st-dismas.archivesportsmouth.com/site/
St. Dismas Guild | https://stdismasguild.org/
St. Dismas Prison Ministry Foundation | www.saintdismas.org/
St. Dismas Prison Ministry Society | www.dismasprisonministry.org/
St. Nicholas Orthodox Church – St. Dismas Prison Ministry |
   www.stnicholasoc.org/prison-ministry/
The Community of St. Dysmas | http://stdysmasmd.org/
Two Saints | www.twosaints.org.uk/

CHARITIES DOING TRANSFORMATIONAL WORK WITH PRISONERS

Fine Cell Work | https://finecellwork.co.uk/
Justice Defenders | www.justice-defenders.org/
Khulisa | www.khulisa.co.uk/
Prisoners' Education Trust | www.prisonerseducation.org.uk/
Prison Fellowship International | https://pfi.org/
Prison Network | http://prisonnetwork.org.au/
Restore | http://restore.org.za/
Switchback | https://switchback.org.uk/
The Clink Charity | https://theclinkcharity.org/

FURTHER READING

A Doctor at Calvary – Pierre Babets (2014, first published in 1953)
A Guide to Christian Art – Diane Apostolos-Cappadona (2020)
Art and the Christian Apocrypha – David R. Cartlidge & J. Keith Elliot (2001)
Augustus – John Buchan (1937)
Augustus: From Revolutionary to Emperor – Adrian Goldsworthy (2020)
Augustus: First Emperor of Rome – Adrian Goldsworthy (2015)
Augustus: The Biography – Jochen Bleiken (1998)
Byzantine Art – Robin Cormack (2018)
Christ the Heart of Creation – Rowan Williams (2018)
Crucifixion – Editors of Phaidon Press (2000)
God Crucified – Richard Bauckham (1998)
Gospel Figures in Art – Stefano Zuffi (2003)
Jerusalem as Jesus Knew It – John Wilkinson (1978)
Jerusalem in the Time of Jesus – Joachim Jeremias (2014, first published in 1969)
Jesus and Judaism – E. P. Sanders (1985)
Le Voleur de Paradis – Christiane Klapisch-Zuber (2015 – In French)
Life of the Good Thief – J. J. Gaume & M. De Lisle (tr) (2003, first published in 1882)
Pilate: The Biography of an Invented Man – Ann Wroe (2010)
Pontius Pilate: Deciphering a Memory – Aldo Schiavone (2017)
Religious Painting: Christ's Passion and Crucifixion – Stephanie Brown (1979)
*Sactity Pictured: The Art of the Dominican and Franciscan Orders
   in Renaissance Italy* – Trinita Kennedy (2014)
Sacred Doorway: A Beginner's Guide to Icons – Linette Martin (2002)
Seeing Salvation: Images of Christ in Art – Neil MacGregor (2000)
Signs and Symbols in Christian Art – George Ferguson (1966)
The Art of the Sacred – Graham Howes (2006)
The Cross of the Son of God – Martin Hegel (1986)
The Crucifixion in American Art – Robert Henkes (2003)
The Crucifixion of Jesus: A Forensic Inquiry – Frederick T. Zugibe (2005)
The Death of the Messiah – Raymond E. Brown (2007)
The Good Thief – André Daigneault (2005)
The Historical Figure of Jesus – E. P. Sanders (1993)
The Memoirs of Pontius Pilate – Carlo Maria Franzero (1961)
The Mystical Language of Icons – Solrunn Nes (2009)
Tiberius – Robin Seager (2005)
Tiberius Caesar: Emperor of Rome – G. P. Baker (2000)
*Two Other Men: Lessons from the Thieves in the Crucifixion Narrative
   of St. Luke* – Graham Reeves (2017)